Wood Engraving

Wood

A Studio Book

Engraving

An Adventure in Printmaking

David M. Sander

The Viking Press   **New York**

Acknowledgments

I am grateful to the many wood engravers who have allowed their works to be reproduced in this book. Every care has been taken to obtain permission and give proper credit but I apologize now for any errors or omissions which, if they exist, are purely unintentional.

I am also grateful for the wood engraving heritage into which I was born and for the memory of my father, who taught me to engrave and to endure. I wish to thank the men of the Sander Wood Engraving Company, whose daily work, largely unknown and unsung, has been the inspiration for much of this book; John De Pol for his enthusiasm; Leonard Baskin for his preface to this volume and for his friendship; Albert Garrett and Kenneth Lindley of Great Britain for their hospitality across the sea; Paul Quirk, Glen Jeskey, Stefan Martin, Paulius Augius, Jonas Tricis, Robert Schranz, and Charles Joslin, whose artistry and craftsmanship have closed the gap between "commercial" and "artistic" wood engraving; R. Hunter Middleton for his latter-day magnificent Bewick proofs and his generosity to me; and the students and faculties at Columbia College of Chicago, Rollins College of Florida, and State College of New York at Buffalo, whose involvement and feedback have given me material and insights for these pages; and a special note of thanks to Martina D'Alton, whose editing has brought this volume to whatever heights it may have achieved.

First published in 1978 by The Viking Press
625 Madison Avenue, New York, N.Y. 10022
Published simultaneously in Canada by
Penguin Books Canada Limited

Library of Congress Cataloging in Publication Data
Sander, David M
  Wood engraving.
  (A Studio book)
  Bibliography: p.
  1. Wood-engraving—Technique.   I. Title.
NE1227.S27   761'.2   78–8097
ISBN 0–670–78083–9

Printed in the United States of America
Set in Caledonia
Book design by Christopher B. Holme

Contents

To Susan Sander and Inara Cedrins
whose faith and help have made this book possible

Preface

One day late in the eighteenth century Thomas Bewick happened to work his engraving burin into the end grain of a piece of hard wood. This was the beginning of a long, fruitful exploration of the tonal range and extraordinary finesse possible in the medium now called wood engraving. Bewick's discovery, which was of great importance, made possible the printing of delicately wrought engravings along with type, and publishers were the first to benefit from the happy accidental find.

Bewick himself grew quite proficient and produced a stream of books illustrated with his startling new wood engravings. He trained others, who in turn trained still other artists, and by the 1880s—that terrifying moment in history when photomechanical reproduction became a reality—there were thousands and thousands of engravers in boxwood working throughout the world. Most of these engravers were artisans executing with supreme skill and dispatch the drawings that the artists drew on boxwood blocks. As photomechanical techniques replaced the beleaguered wood engravers, the medium was reborn in the hands of the artists themselves, who discovered in the highly polished flintlike substance of Turkish boxwood the adumbration of a new and personal medium. For the first time since Bewick these phoenix-artists engraved their own designs. I am impelled to cite their names—Charles Picketts, C. H. Shannon, William Nicholson, Edward Gordon Craig, Lucien Pissarro, Thomas Sturge-Moore, Auguste Lepère, and others both mute and ignoble.

For me, the wood engraving's vital quality lies in the complex of lines, wonderfully fine and sharp, and blazing in blackness on a white ground. I have engraved some two hundred blocks and am even now sensible of the delicious feeling of moving a graver through the refractory, resistant boxwood.

One applauds David Sander's efforts to rekindle the love for craft with its intimate relationship between artist and tool. This noble graphic medium is most deserving of resuscitation, and the artist, having once made a wood engraving, will not leave off for very long.

LEONARD BASKIN

Introduction

As a small child I was often taken downtown to "Daddy's office," where my father operated a commercial wood-engraving company. Since 1919 our shop had been on the seventh floor of a building in the middle of Chicago's printing district. On the street below deliverymen were everywhere, carrying type forms from typesetter to printer and printer to electrotyper, or delivering skids of paper and five-gallon cans of ink to the letterpress printers whose shops lined the street. In the elevators there was always someone carrying proofs or type or rubber stamps. The smell of ink permeated the air, and the sound of presses vibrated from all the buildings.

In our shop a dozen engravers sat by the windows and silently zipped away at their woodblocks, blowing the chips from in front of the tool as they bent to the task, their elbows sticking out from their bodies as they curved a line on the block. The sound of the router came from the toolroom as backgrounds were removed from the block. The arc lamp hissed occasionally from the photographer's room as he put another image on yet another block.

The pictures we made were unlike anything I had seen before or since, an entirely different breed of illustration. They were not in my schoolbooks or in books at the library; they were in newspapers now and then, and in catalogues, and here and there in magazines; and every time my father brought one of these publications home, I could see that the boldness and excitement in our pictures were missing in almost everything from other print shops.

One day, at sixteen, I was sent to pick up some jewelry from a customer. The jeweler spread out a dozen rings on the glass counter of his shop and asked, "How much are you going to charge to do these rings?" Never having been asked that question, I guessed that we would charge about five dollars each. At that the jeweler scooped them back into the bag and said, "I can get a halftone made for three." My father later explained that we were competing against a machine, and shrugged as if to say "That's the way it is." Commercial wood engraving was to lose the battle.

When I came back from World War II, I entered my father's business. I knew how effectively our wood engravings reproduced products in newspaper advertisements, and I set about getting that kind of work. When we did a piece of catalogue jewelry, we were merely another kind of reproduction process, and the little engraving companies around us that had once thrived on catalogue work were closing day by day, unable to meet the competition. But when we made newspaper product illustrations for advertising agencies, we were creating *artwork,* making pictures out of lines the same way other artists did. As I took over the management of our company, I began to train apprentices who were already artists, most of them graduates of the Art Institute or the American Academy in Chicago, and all of them bringing a vital new force to wood engraving and to my father's shop.

We soon picked up a lot of newspaper advertising illustration. I chanced to talk to an art director one afternoon whose agency had just gotten the Motorola account, and for three years our little company made every Motorola television set in three sizes for newspaper dealer mats. For a time every newspaper in America had some of our Motorolas in it. Then we did Wrigley's Spearmint chewing gum, which appeared on newspaper comic pages in hundreds of cities; and when I called on art directors to sell them wood-engraving artwork—that's what it was and that's what I called it—I used to show them their local paper. No matter what city I was in, there were always three or four different Sander wood engravings in the local papers, each one bold and clear. We took our company to advertising trade shows. During several shows in New York City one of our

engravers demonstrated wood engraving in full view of ten thousand passing advertising executives.

Even after the death of my father I did not realize that wood engraving was fast becoming a lost art, that it was about to vanish from the commercial scene. We were still making thirty or forty wood engravings a week. When we were busy, however, we often had difficulty finding engravers. Many of our old friends in Chicago had either retired to Florida or died. We tried to bring in engravers from other American cities and found none left. We tried abroad, but they had vanished from England, Germany, France, and Japan, too.

Then one day we were offered some original Thomas Bewick blocks from the estate of Ben Abramson, a Chicago bookseller. We purchased three hundred of those that had been used in printing Bewick's five-volume memorial edition of *Birds, Fishes, Quadrupeds, Fables,* and his pictureless *Memoir.*

Almost overnight I became interested in the history of wood engraving, and only then did I realize the historical importance of our company as the last commercial shop left.

I began to collect books about wood engraving, and to learn, so to speak, the names of the players. Leonard Baskin came to visit our shop, never having seen commercial wood engraving. So did Claire

Leighton, who was so impressed with our reproductive skills that she importuned her publisher to add three pages of our work to her book on wood engraving, then already at the printer's.

In our shop we did so many different kinds of wood engraving that we had to invent new techniques almost every week. Advertising agencies began to ask us for pictorial illustrations, university presses for book illustrations, and specialty printers came to us to solve their illustrating problems. It became an irony repeated at frequent intervals that this hundred-and-fifty-year-old process was often the only one that would work in making pictures for the newest giant presses and the latest technical innovations. For a time wood engraving was the only way to make illustrations in several colors directly on corrugated boxboard, and every packaging magazine wrote long illustrated articles about our work.

In 1971 I spent three days, by invitation, at the art department at Rollins College in Florida showing the students how to make wood engravings. Three days! Our own apprentice program took four years, and the first six weeks were spent doing nothing but practicing parallel lines! But at Rollins something exciting happened; from the first morning session the students themselves were very excited, and many came back to work on their own in the afternoon, some even skipping other classes. They worked in

In the 1950s our company produced this engraving, which appeared in virtually every daily newspaper throughout the country. Wrigley's art director recognized and preferred the quality of the engraving shading—especially on the gum package.

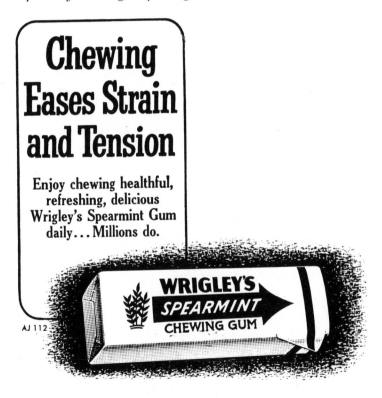

the halls, on the stairs, whenever they had a free moment. The second day saw even more students joining the class, and a few members of the art department faculty as well. By the third day the print room was crowded to overflowing with both students and faculty. It was beginning to dawn on me that wood engraving could be "learned" in twenty minutes, the time it took one student to show another how to hold the tool and to draw a pencil picture on the woodblock.

I returned from Rollins with the clear idea that wood engraving could have a glorious rebirth. I envisioned art departments in colleges teaching wood engraving as they now teach silk screen or stone lithography or woodblock printing. It could even be taught in high schools.

I set to work and learned from my Rollins experience. The students had used only the tools which I had shortened rather than the long ones; they had had me sharpen the tools because we had no sharpening jigs; and they had been forced to stand in lines at the presses.

Finding that not a single engraving tool company made short tools, I designed some new ones with nice curved bellies and went to the tool companies to have them made. No one would make them. "We have been doing it our way for seventy-five years," they said. Pursued by my dream and unable to stop, I decided to have the tools specially made. Then I found a sharpening jig that worked very nicely and could be used in a classroom; next I designed a simple proofing jig that works just fine.

My small catalogue of supplies and instructions went out to schools and hobbyists in 1972, and since then hundreds of schools have ordered it and have begun wood-engraving programs. Other hundreds of individuals have also ordered materials and made wood engravings.

When I began reading the various books on how to make wood engravings, I found they all suffered from a major flaw. Each had been written by a nationally known engraver in England or America, and each was a slim volume devoted to showing how that engraver went about making the breathtaking and beautiful life work for which he or she was known. Some were printed directly from the original blocks. The flaw, if I may call it that, lay in their approach. Readers were made to feel that wood engraving was an esoteric art and a difficult one to learn, and that between beginning and mastering the art lay many years of assiduous practice. There seemed to be no middle ground between rank amateurs and fine art. Furthermore, the authors often contradicted one another, and all of them, despite their great insight and talent, had limited experience with other engravers or techniques.

It seemed that for engraving to become widely practiced, a book had to be written that would encompass *all* techniques—commercial and artistic—and talk about wood engraving as one would talk about cooking or carpentry, not as an art pursued by the gods but as a craft practiced in everyday life.

Hence this volume. While it does not lay bare the work of every great engraver of the past, it contains the techniques that I have demonstrated in workshops throughout the country, from university art departments to junior high school art rooms. In fact, I have watched people eagerly making wood engravings in such diverse places as student union lobbies, bookstore counters, train stations, women's clubs, and art fairs. One of my most joyful experiences was in a class of junior high school eleven- and twelve-year-olds. The children drew and engraved pictures by the end of the first hour, and then gathered around the press, proofing five or six blocks at a time, and trading prints excitedly until nearly every pupil had a proof of every block.

In the not too distant future blocks and tools for wood engraving may be sold in every art and hobby store, and schools at all grade levels may teach wood engraving as they now teach linoleum block printing.

I hope that this little book, the first to propose wood engraving as a hobby or career for practically everybody, will help bring the joy of wood engraving to many, and my dream a little closer to reality.

1 A Brief History of Wood Engraving

In the past century hundreds of books have been written on aspects of wood engraving, and tens of thousands of books have been illustrated with wood engravings. Today, however, almost none of this literature can be found in art stores or libraries. Once in a while an old history of the art turns up in a second-hand bookstore or in the print department of a major museum, but these seem to misunderstand what wood engraving is and to record the errors of previous histories.

I once heard a student at a Midwestern university ask the instructor in modern art when they were going to get beyond Paul Cézanne. "We are not going past Cézanne," the instructor said, "because beyond Cézanne nothing is certain." That seems to be the way with wood-engraving histories. Few continue past Thomas Bewick. They devote most of their attention to Egyptian cuneiform writing, Chinese playing cards of the fifth century, block prints from the time of Gutenberg, and prints of Cranach the Elder and Albrecht Dürer, comment briefly on the engravings of Holbein and William Blake, and conclude with a chapter on Thomas Bewick (1753–1828), who was the only one of the entire group who even made true wood engravings!

Looking backward in time from the hundreds of marvelously illustrated books of wood engravings published in England and America during the 1940s, to the wood-engraving societies and their fabled print exhibitions in the 1930s, to the tens of thousands of magazines, newspapers, catalogues, broadsides, and books illustrated in wood by the commercial engravers of the last half of the nineteenth century, we wonder at the phenomenon—how it came about, who invented it, and why it disappeared.

There are really two founders of wood engraving as we know it today. One was the Industrial Revolution, which shook civilization out of the way of life it had known for thousands of years, and the other was Thomas Bewick, who lived at that certain time and in that certain place.

He was born in 1753, and before he was twenty his contemporary James Watt was already making steam engines to suck water from the deep Scottish mines, while Richard Arkwright was perfecting the spinning jennies that would shortly do the work of almost a thousand men and take weavers from farms and set them to work in city factories. Benjamin Franklin, with his famous kite, had long since discovered electricity in lightning; and English coke, made from coal, was heating iron mills and foundries all over Great Britain.

Bewick himself became part of this new mechanical ingeniousness at the age of fourteen, when he apprenticed himself to an engraver who made all the ornaments and carvings on swords, guns, doorknobs, and the like in the small town of Newcastle-on-Tyne, near Bewick's birthplace. Bewick, who had shown an aptitude for art from his earliest childhood, was put to work cutting pictures and ornaments on all manner of metal and wood. In the process he devised the very tools he used.

It was not long before he had engraved pictures for several printers, and he found that, unlike wood slabs cut with the grain, end-grain wood permitted cutting easily in all directions, and that Turkish boxwood was the best wood for the task. Certain kinds of tools were required to make the closely spaced lines, and Bewick designed these tools. He did all this not as an inventor in a laboratory, but as an artisan seeking a way of doing his job a little better, of creating something that would solve the immediate problem at hand.

Bewick was soon doing all the block-cutting in the establishment, and had illustrated several technical books. He had begun to formulate another element of modern wood engraving—a whole new vocabulary of shading, which has been part of every wood engraving made ever since.

From Quadrupeds, *drawn and engraved by Thomas Bewick.*

What he had invented was a new form of artistic expression, and a new kind of printing plate. Together they would become the principal method of illustrating virtually every book, newspaper, magazine, catalogue, flyer, and broadside printed for a hundred years after his death. His practices are still followed today by everyone who makes wood engravings.

Bewick's method of shading was revolutionary. Other artisans had used end-grain wood for various printing purposes. The Frenchman J. L. Papillon, who wrote a treatise on wood engraving, had executed designs and flourishes on boxwood with tools similar to Bewick's many years before. But until Bewick, everyone who cut pictures into wood drew

From British Birds, *drawn and engraved by Thomas Bewick.*

them first on the block with pen and ink, and then merely cut from the wood all the areas between the drawn lines.

Bewick saw wood engraving as one continuous act from the drawing on the wood in soft pencil to the completion of the final lines. He drew to engrave; he engraved to demonstrate, to breathe life into the picture he was making. To keep the act of engraving meaningful and creative, he interpreted the soft pencil tones with a line structure that was quick, easy, adaptable to all subject matter, capable of infinite variation, and contained within the lines the vitality of the engraver's identity and feelings.

Instead of thinking of the surface of the block as white on which black lines were to be drawn, Bewick thought of the block as black and the lines as white, used to lighten the areas that were not meant to be black. His tones were composed of white lines, his textures were white lines, all in a kind of shorthand to get his ideas onto the block as rapidly as possible. His wood engravings were not done in haste, to be sure, but to do them in his new, sensitive white-line technique was to complete them much faster and much more creatively than if they had been drawn in ink on the block, with black lines hatching across each other as the sole shading technique. To cut out cross-hatching is an impersonal act, one of removing little bits of wood as perfectly as possible. Then the engraver is not concerned with the idea of the drawing. In fact, the act is so laborious that no personal or interpretive concern is possible. Through Bewick's work the white line was born, or reborn, if indeed it had been used occasionally before him.

Bewick set about illustrating, from his personal observation, a natural history of quadrupeds, which he completed in 1789 and printed in an edition of one thousand. It soon sold out, and went through eight editions in Bewick's lifetime. He followed *Quadrupeds* with two books of British birds and an *Aesop's Fables* before he died in 1828. His memoir, completed in his lifetime, was not printed until long after his death.

Like every other book in the world at that time, Bewick's work was printed on a wooden press. A leather inking ball was "dabbed" first on an inked surface and then on the type and woodblocks until the whole printing surface was thought sufficiently blacked. The type and wood engravings were locked together so that they would not move about, covered by a paper, and slid under the flat platen of the press, which closed by a lever that turned a wooden screw.

Through this laborious process three good men, working continuously and hard, could produce about sixty impressions an hour on one side of a sheet of paper. That was in 1790.

By the time of Bewick's death in 1828 giant cylinder presses with curved metal plates were printing newspapers many pages at a time at the rate of five thousand impressions an hour. The illustrated weekly newspapers followed shortly after, and the deluge had begun.

During Bewick's lifetime had come the cast-iron steam-powered presses, the gelatin rollers that could spread ink evenly over a bed of type and woodcuts three and four feet wide, abundant paper, newly literate readers by the hundreds of thousands, and a whole new breed of men and women who worked in their homes and small shops all day peering through magnifying glasses at small blocks of wood and cutting the pictures that illuminated an entire century. These were the commercial engravers.

Bewick himself was the first teacher, and his pupils went on to teach others in other cities and countries. But Bewick's work itself was probably the best teacher, and his books were widely known and read throughout the civilized world. John James Audubon, the great American naturalist, visited Bewick, the great British naturalist, in his later years, and they became friends and shared their insights. Wordsworth wrote a sonnet to Bewick. Known during his lifetime as one of the great English artists, he continues to inspire other artists. Bewick's belongings were enshrined long after his death by his family and friends. All of his blocks for *Quadrupeds, Land Birds, Water Birds, and Fables* were reprinted together with his *Memoir* in 1878. The very chair in which he worked spent its last years displayed on a pedestal in the middle of a great London wood-engraving company.

Rear view of a nineteenth century block, showing the manner in which many small blocks were bolted together.

For Bewick, wood engraving had been a means to an end; he had used his drawing ability and his wood-engraving skill to create the things he had to say. But with the advent of widespread printing and the enormous demand for pictures, the artist/engraver was no longer a practical combination. Draughtsmen who could depict shipwrecks, landscapes, portraits, natural wonders, catastrophes, and everything else that was handed to them by their employers drew pictures on whitened boxwood. Others who could best imitate previous engraving techniques actually cut the pictures into the wood.

In the larger shops engravers had their specialties, and a single block was often worked on by several men. One would do faces, another clothing, a third backgrounds. In the 1850s a machine was invented that would cut grooves into the back of the woodblock so that many small blocks could be bolted together while the drawing was being made and then separated for engraving by different engravers. It was rejoined with nuts and bolts at the finish, and a master engraver would make the final lines over the now invisible joint. The result was to all appearances the effort of a single engraver. In the first issue of *The London Illustrated News* it was advertised that more than sixty engravers had worked to create a single double-page spread.

Almost from the beginning Bewick's work was known in America and widely copied here. Our most famous early wood engraver, Alexander Anderson, copied on wood an early edition of an English book illustrated by John Bewick, Thomas's brother. Anderson himself had many pupils, and by the 1830s the so-called white-line wood engraving of Thomas Bewick had been adopted internationally as the best method of shading the ever increasing number of blocks.

The London Illustrated News was followed by *Harper's Monthly*, and then *Harper's Weekly,* both in the United States. Soon there were "illustrated" weekly newspapers in cities everywhere and every large city in America and Europe had a cluster of wood-engraving shops and specialty shops where wood engravings could be "plugged" to correct slips, alterations, or bad seams and old blocks could be resurfaced so they could be used again and again. There were factories that made type-high boxwood blocks and wood-engraving tools. There were schools that taught men how to engrave and special schools to teach women. In the years when wood engraving was at its height an estimated four to five thousand persons practiced the trade. Most of them worked at home, but many found jobs in lofts with large windows where they could work by natural light.

Wood engraving was never the only way to make printed illustrations. Stone lithography and copper (later supplanted by steel) engravings were widely used from about 1820 on to illustrate books of all kinds. The virtue of wood engraving was that woodblocks were also letterpress plates and could be locked up with type on any kind of press that printed from raised surfaces. Stone lithography and steel and copper etchings had to be printed on different kinds of presses, and the prints had to be glued or sewn into publications that printed letterpress.

It's hardly surprising that virtually all the illustrated matter of the first eight decades of the nineteenth century was wood engraving. Evidence from library shelves and old bookstores may seem to indicate the contrary, but we must remember that most wood engravings were ephemeral and have been lost to us in the countless newspapers and broadsides that were printed on perishable newsprint paper and thrown away.

Even so, it is very easy for a novice at printing history to become an "expert" on wood engraving. If a book has illustrations in it, if it was printed before about 1880, and if the illustrations appear on the same page as the type, one can say with certainty that these pictures are wood engravings. Even if they look like etchings, pen drawings, or lithographs (wood engravers often imitated these techniques on wood), only wood engravings could be printed with the type.

Then, in the 1880s, a new phenomenon appeared. Photography had been used for at least thirty years to put images on the woodblock for

Left: *Halftone illustration.* Right: *Wood engraving.*
*The clarity and amount of detail in the engraving made
this process the first choice of advertisers for decades.*

engravers to cut, but now a method was discovered
to put the photographic image onto a metal plate
and etch the image with acid. This produced a printing plate that required no handwork at all. At first
this new method, called "photoengraving," was used
only for black pen drawings on white paper, but
soon a dot-patterned screen was invented to trans-
late the tones of a photograph, drawing, or painting
into dots. Each dot printed solid black, and by varying the size of the dots, the kinds of tones that had
been made by the wood engraver with thick or thin
lines were created.

The era of commercial wood engraving was over,
although it was many decades before reproductive
engraving came to a complete halt. A 1900 census
listed 145 wood-engraving companies in the United
States.

Photoengraving has always had some inade-
quacies, especially when compared with wood engraving. The photoengraving screen renders *everything* into dots, so that the deep blacks and pure
whites of the original drawing or photograph become
dark gray and light gray, and the visual excitement
of pure black and pure white is completely lost. Fine
detail and sharp lines are reduced to an irresolute
wavy group of dots, and the absolute clarity of the
wood engraving is lost. Magazine editors, conscious
of this loss of contrast and clarity in their new illustrations, hired the out-of-work wood engravers to re-
store what they could to the copper and zinc plates. A

whole new trade, "photofinishing," was created, and early photoengravings show the deliberate marks of the wood engravers' tools as they tried vainly to add interest to a lackluster sky or highlight an otherwise drab face or dress.

Photoengravings, now called "halftones," are made in various screens to suit the paper on which they are printed. Fine enamel stock will take a two hundred-screen halftone (meaning two hundred dots to the inch), while the exigencies of letterpress newspaper production require that there be no more than a fifty- or fifty-five-screen used. If you pick up a large metropolitan daily newspaper, you can see how difficult it is to get clarity, detail, or contrast in editorial photographs or advertisements.

The modern wood engraver has at least one tool that Bewick never envisioned—the multiple-line tool. This was created for the halftone finisher so that a half-dozen or so lines could be "cleaned out" in a single stroke. It is made in all the halftone screen sizes from about sixteen lines per inch to two hundred or more.

There was another addition to the modern engraver's bag of tricks, and that was the ruling machine, a mechanical device created in the 1880s to rule straight, perfect parallel lines. It could go from thin to thick and thin again while still retaining the structure of so many lines per inch. This machine

was used exclusively for the illustrations of various machines, threads, cylinders, and the like. It was widely employed by commercial engravers to make those parts of each product illustration that required this exactness. The ruling machine was often quite complex, although even the most complicated ruled only one line at a time, guided entirely by the whim of the operator. Some had wave bars, against which the engraving tool was pressed as it made its stroke, and a series of wavy lines could be made. Concentric circles could also be cut, as could diverging and

The ruling machine.

converging lines. Combinations of these lines produced borders very similar to those used on checks, stocks, bonds, and currency. I've collected more than a dozen of these interesting machines over the years.

While wood engraving was seldom used for editorial illustration after the invention of the halftones,

The Sander Wood Engraving Company in the 1950s. Five ruling machines are in view, two of them in use.

it continued to be in great demand for highly detailed products that were printed on newsprint paper. Advertisements in newspapers, product illustrations in mail-order catalogues, and quality work in many magazines kept hundreds of engravers in business well into the twentieth century. Chicago, where the largest mail-order catalogues of Sears, Montgomery Ward, and many other companies were printed, became the commercial wood-engraving capital of the world. Some shops had as many as fifty engravers. There were at least a half-dozen large shops, with perhaps another half-dozen smaller ones. At the Chicago Wood Engravers Union Picnic, in 1925, more than a hundred members were present.

New printing processes such as rotogravure permitted great detail to be printed photomechanically, and one by one the wood-engraving shops closed their doors. Soon there were only a handful of engravers working in Chicago, and all of them in the single remaining shop, The Sander Engraving Company owned by my father. We often tried to find commercial engravers, first in other American cities, and then in countries around the world, but by 1950 we could find none. Even so our shop was an active one, engraving pictures of scientific apparatus, automobile parts, aerial views of industrial plants, portraits, breeds of dogs, and many more. Much of this was for catalogues and technical publications, and occasionally for book illustration.

While commercial wood engravers had been plying their trade, a new kind of wood engraver had

Page from a typical mail-order catalogue of the 1920s. This one was printed in England.

emerged whose work appeared in the pages of such celebrated American magazines as *The Century*, *Harper's Monthly*, and their English counterparts. These wood engravers signed their work in the block, and in many cases they drew as well as en-

An elegant wood engraving of an equally elegant subject. The lines are very fine and the shading exquisite.

graved their own pictures. They and the magazines that employed them considered wood engraving a

My father, Jacob Sander, engraved this clothing advertisement in the early 1920s. The original painting was by Francis Xavier Leyendecker, whose brother Joseph Christian designed many covers for the Saturday Evening Post.

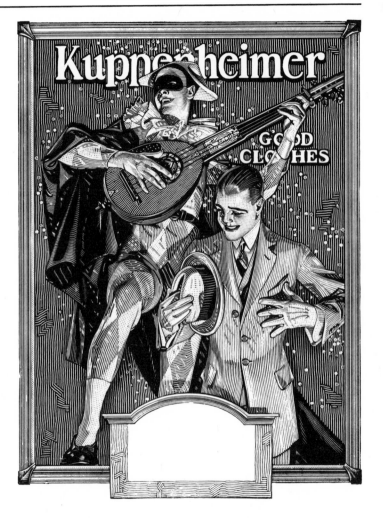

fine art like painting or sculpture. Articles, symposia, letters to the editor, and editorials of the period all attest to the great advances shown by these wood engravings and to the virtuosity of the well-known men (there were no women in this elite group yet) who made theim. A. V. S. Anthony, Timothy Cole, Frederick Juengling, W. J. Linton, and Henry Wolf won prizes at prestigious print shows, and proofs of their work sold for fine prices to art collectors. A show in 1889 at the Grolier Club in New York City contained 259 proofs by 25 wood engravers. Its nucleus was the American contribution to the Paris Exposition, where it won for American engravers "enviable honors," according to *Harper's Monthly*, from the International Jury of Awards for the Fine Art section. Even before the Exposition major American museums like the Boston Museum of Fine Arts and The National Museum at Washington had shown what was being done in this branch of the art.

One American wood engraver, Elbridge Kingsley, basking in the glory of the great demand for his work by such important magazines, as *The Century*, had his own railroad car complete with beds, kitchen, and tables at the windows at the proper height for wood engraving. He and his cronies took

These engravings demonstrate the elegance and fine detail given to almost every subject — even a bathroom.

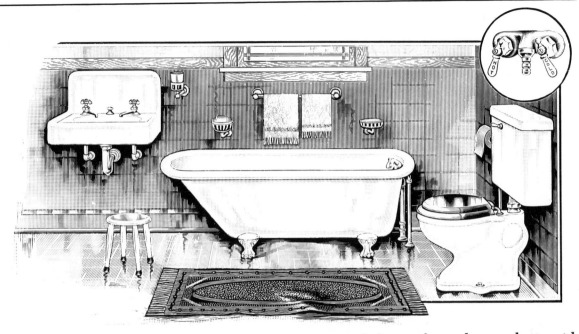

regular outings in the country, and with the car shunted off onto a siding they sketched and engraved the wonders of nature while comfortably looking out the windows at whatever weather the gods chose to bestow.

During the 1880s a popular children's magazine offered prizes to its readers for getting subscriptions. In addition to a fishing pole, tennis racket, and camera, one of the prizes was a wood-engraving kit. Wood-engraving kits were offered for sale in many adult magazines as well, alongside the ads for typewriters and "electric salve." At the Ford Museum

near Detroit one of the artifacts shown along with the Wright Brothers' bicycle shop and newspaper office is a wood engraver's kit of several tools in a wooden box—a present from Orville to Wilbur.

Because wood engraving was often done at home even for the largest clients, it was frequently thought of as an ideal occupation for women. A number of schools were established in the United States and in England to train women in that art, and magazines often editorialized about the virtues of the trade for girls and young ladies desirous of improving their lot. But for the most part women played no role in wood engraving until the 1920s. Since then, the list of women engravers, particularly in England, is almost as long as that of the men.

By 1893, the time of the Columbian Exposition in Chicago, wood engraving was no longer employed for editorial illustration, although it appeared in the advertisements in *Harper's* and other magazines until long after the turn of the century. The glorious era had vanished, not to be revived until the 1920s, and then in a completely different form.

In England in 1904 two art students, Lucien Pissarro and Noel Rooke, began making multicolor wood engravings and woodblock prints. Rooke was later appointed teacher of book illustration at the Central School of Arts and Crafts and began to teach wood engraving there in 1912. Eric Gill, a student friend of Rooke's in 1904, published one of the first two books said to contain modern wood engravings drawn and engraved by a single artist in the new style—the other was published by Gwendolen Raverat.

By 1920 there was enough interest in this new wood engraving to form the Society of Wood Engravers. There were ten original members, gathered together by Gill. The roster included Edward Gordon Craig, E. M. O'R. Dickey, Robert Gibbings, Gill, Philip Hagreen, Sydney Lee, John Nash, Lucien Pissarro, Gwendolen Raverat, and Noel Rooke.

Their first group exhibition in 1920 raised £268 through the sale of their work. This must have been considered quite satisfactory, especially since many of the prints were unframed. All ten of these engravers received international acclaim in later years.

The 1920 exhibition did two remarkable things for wood engraving. It legitimized the wood-engraving print as socially desirable and worthy of collecting alongside lithographs, drawings, and etchings; and it introduced a whole new genre of wood engraving, quite different from all that had preceded it.

The new wood engraving had none of the shadings and tones of the hundred years that had passed since Bewick, none of the virtuosity of the Lintons, Dalziels, and Swains who had engraved the book illustrations of the 70s, 80s, and 90s. Here was a whole new use of the end-grain block. These new artist/engravers created a visual austerity with large

From The Sun, *a novel in woodcut by Frans Masereel.*

masses of black against large masses of white—almost silhouettes in many cases, with just a little shading at the edges for relief.

From this new beginning, in less than a decade there were anywhere from a hundred to a thousand wood engravers in every country in the Western world. Exhibitions and competitions were held in the international salons. The day of Bewick, when one artist conceived, drew, engraved, and proofed his or her own blocks, had returned once more, this time to stay.

By 1927 a number of British publishers had produced books in which the illustrations were wood engravings commissioned by the publisher. The most important figure during that period was the engraver Robert Gibbings, who in 1924 acquired a small book publishing firm, renamed it The Golden Cockerel Press, and for ten years commissioned wood engravings for dozens of books and personally supervised

their printing. They were the delight of bibliophiles everywhere. By 1931 his editions were sold out a year in advance. Being more an artist than a businessman, however, he foreswore the enterprise, and since 1934 has illustrated other people's books. The Golden Cockerel Press continued under other supervision to publish similar works.

The list of Golden Cockerel engravers is long and worthy, an impressive group that has inspired other engravers to this very day. Among the number are Dorothea Braby, John Buckland-Wright, Gibbings, Eric Gill, Blair Hughes-Stanton, John Nash's brother Paul, Eric Ravilious, Mark Severin, Reynolds Stone, Clifford Webb, and John Farleigh.

While I cannot attempt to list all the superb British wood engravers of the 1920s and 1930s, I will mention Claire Leighton, Iain Macnab, Agnes Miller Parker, C. F. Tunnicliffe, Douglas Percy Bliss, and Gertrude Hermes. To Britain belongs the envi-

able credit for having twice created wood engraving as we know it today—once almost two hundred years ago and again early in this century.

In America the Second International Exhibition of Lithography and Wood Engraving at the Art Institute of Chicago in 1931 showed wood engravings from Argentina, Australia, Austria, Belgium, Canada, Czechoslovakia, France, Holland, Ireland, Italy, Japan, Poland, Russia, Spain, Sweden, Switzerland, and the United States. Many artists whose international fame derives from their painting or sculpture made wood engravings during the 1930s—Josef Albers, Hans Arp, Ernst Barlach, Aristide Maillol, Georges Rouault, and Rufino Tamayo, to name only a few.

Special mention must be made of Frans Masereel of Belgium, who created in the 1920s several widely "read" novels entirely of pictures, every page increasing the intensity of the story. While his novels, several of which have been reprinted, were woodblock prints and not wood engravings, they helped arouse international interest in wood engraving and may have inspired the German artist Otto Nückel and the American Lynd Ward.

The United States produced many artist/engravers whose prints were widely prized. The Albany Print Club and the Woodcut Society of Kansas City —there were undoubtedly many others—created a membership of interested buyers for whom the clubs

From God's Man, *a novel in wood by Lynd Ward, 1929.*

From Otto Nückel's novel, Destiny, 1930. Because of the scarcity of woodblocks in Germany after World War I, Nückel painstakingly engraved on lead blocks to create this story of social ills.

Jacob Sander, Bookplate. *My father has engraved his name in the lower right corner, followed by "del," which is the old abbreviation for artist, and "sc" for sculptor, as engravers were once called.*

would commission entire editions of prints and send them out to members on a regular basis. J. J. Lankes, Asa Cheffetz, and Thomas Nason did much to articulate the breadth and beauty of the American landscape. Lankes' wood engravings were used for many years to illustrate the editions of poetry by Robert Frost. At international print shows would be engravings by Rockwell Kent, Lynd Ward, Rudolph Ruzicka, Charles Turzak, Nason, Paul Landacre, Leo Meissner, Wanda Gág, Cheffetz, and Frederick Larson.

In the early 1940s Random House published a series of literary classics. In 1941 *Don Quixote* was illustrated in wood by Hans Alexander Mueller, and in 1943 Fritz Eichenberg illustrated *Jane Eyre.* The new editions brought great attention to the work of the two wood engravers who have contributed heavily to the advancement of wood engraving in America. Eichenberg was for years the graphics head of Pratt Institute in New York City, and continues to exhibit in one-man shows. Mueller published his own book, *How I Make Woodcuts and Wood Engravings,* in 1945.

Unlike in Great Britain, where Blair Hughes-Stanton, now in his seventies, has been teaching wood engraving for five decades at the Central School, the several dozen wood engravers of this country taught only a few carefully chosen students. Misch Kohn taught at the Chicago Institute of Design on the Illinois Institute of Technology campus, Leonard Baskin at Smith, Adrian Troy at the Art Institute of Chicago, and Rudolph Ruzicka at Dartmouth College. These men and a few others like them have sustained whatever breadth wood engraving has had in the last thirty years.

National print exhibitions during the last three decades have usually had one or two wood engravings, but print galleries in major cities almost never show wood engravings. Naturally, there have been success stories, but they are exceptions. A high-salaried art director for a well-known advertising agency in New York, Bernard Brussel-Smith, gave up his lucrative job in the 1940s because he fell in love with wood engraving and wanted to spend his life at this practice. His work appeared in many national advertisements and in the editorial pages of *Life* magazine.

There are today probably no more than fifty Americans who illustrate books or send prints to exhibitions, and this book wouldn't be complete if I didn't mention a few of them. Among them are Charles Joslin, Erwin Bergdoll, Bernard Solomon, John Bischof, Fred Brian, Inara Cedrins, Frank Eckmair, Leon Gilmour, Elgas Grim, Boyd Hanna, An-

A fine print by Kenneth Lindley, a British engraver whose work as book illustrator and whose exhibitions have helped to revive the art in England today.

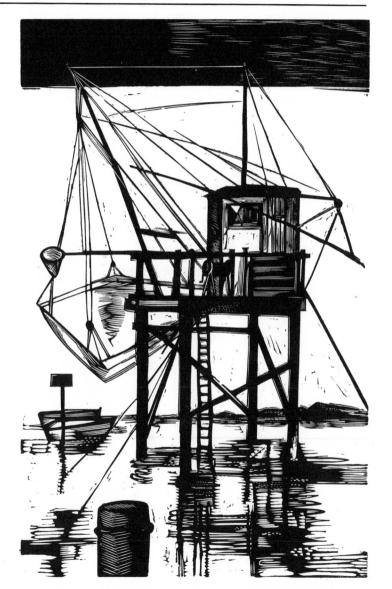

drij Maday, Robert Morrison, Barry Moser, Earl Nitsche, Phillip Reed, John Craig, Robert Billings, Helen Siegl, Jacob Landau, Nora Unwin, Judith Jaidlinger, Fred Becker, Gillian Tyler, and Diane Barr.

From Canada comes the work of G. Brender à Brandis and Rosemary Kilbourn, both of whom are very popular at print shows in that country. Kilbourn, at her own show in a Toronto gallery in 1976, sold every one of her prints, nearly a hundred, and an entire edition of the private-press book she had illustrated.

While there are not many practitioners of wood engraving, the interest continues to be high. My own gallery in Porter, Indiana, carries works by most living American and Canadian wood engravers, and many of the famous engravers of the recent past.

In 1975 The Smithsonian Institution prepared a traveling exhibition of American woodcuts and wood engravings that toured major university art museums. Entitled "American Prints from Wood," it provided a historical survey from the early prints of Anderson to the contemporary work of Baskin and others.

In Chicago a dedicated typophile, R. Hunter Middleton, has for years painstakingly reprinted limited editions of his own collection of Bewick blocks and those of the Newberry Library of Chicago. Each print lives again in fresh luminosity, incidentally proving that none of the Bewick blocks have even slightly diminished in splendor since their original printing two hundred years ago.

In England Albert Garrett, president of the Society of Wood Engravers, has written a book about the wood engravings of Iain Macnab, whose work was widely exhibited in the 1930s. He has also just completed a vast history of British wood engraving.

In New York the wood engravings of Fritz Eichenberg have been given a recent exhibition by the Associated Artists gallery, and John De Pol's work has received renewed attention since his exhibition at the South Street Seaport Museum in lower Manhattan, a museum that contains not only a complete and operating nineteenth-century print shop, open to the public, but also a row of historical proofing presses, all in working order, including an Albion, a Columbian, and several variations of the Washington press.

Baskin's Gehenna Press continues to print small editions of interesting classics with wood-engraving illustrations, and there are more than a half-dozen other small printer/publishers who employ the work of talented new wood engravers. Dover Publications has republished Masereel, and other publishers have commissioned books with wood engravings as the sole illustrations. The new small private presses, some of them with fifty or more books on their list, are among the chief users of wood engravings today.

But by far the major interest in wood engraving is in practicing the craft itself. Art students are taught about wood engraving as part of art history, and teachers and practicing printmakers have long known about the craft. Those of you reading this book will occupy a very special place in the history of wood engraving. You are the next chapter, as yet unwritten, as you take up the craft and turn it to your own devices. It is your involvement that will evoke interest in future years; your prints that will win highest honors in exhibitions, and perhaps grace the walls of museums and galleries throughout the world. It is your new techniques and inspiration that will take wood engraving on to new heights.

Now, begin.

The craft is easy to learn, inexpensive to enjoy, rewarding to practice, and delightful to behold. It can be done by young and old, male and female, as a therapy for the mind as well as the body. It is enjoyable from the first cutting of the first line, and it permits a range of creativity without limitation. It rewards the diligent, the plodder, the talented, and even the artless—each finding in the cutting of the block a special reward.

Have you ever seen a tree so beautifully articulated as this lyrical and stately masterpiece done two hundred years ago by Thomas Bewick?

2 The Wood

The physical act of engraving on wood can be a great pleasure. As the sharp tool clicks away in the wood and clean lines multiply on the block, a smooth, unbroken surface is transformed into a finished illustration. The wood-engraving experience, if you have the right wood, proper tools, and a little training, is a powerful one during which time passes swiftly and productively.

Boxwood is the traditional wood of the wood engraver. It is manufactured in dense, smooth, unblemished slabs with upper surfaces that are perfectly polished, making the blocks pleasant to feel and hold. Sizes vary greatly, but boxwood slabs can be obtained as large as twelve by twelve inches, or in special cases twelve by twenty-four inches. Because the wood will be used for printing or proofing after the drawing has been completed, the slab is manufactured to the same height as metal type—.918 inch.

The most important characteristic of this wood is that it is made from ends of the wood grain, part of a cross section of the tree. The surface of the slab shows the growth rings of the tree, and by counting them we can sometimes tell how old the tree was when it was cut down. A single slab is actually composed of many small blocks that have been glued together so perfectly that none of the joints will appear when the slab is inked or proofed. The wood itself is never a visible part of the engraving as it often is in the other woodblock media.

This perfection, which is possible only in an end-grain slab, is a tribute to the painstaking art of the blockmaker. It permits the wood engraver to make those beautiful pictures that are unique to engraving and distinguishes the technique from the other kinds of block printing—the linoleum cut and the woodcut.

Because the working surface of end-grain wood is uniform in all directions, the engraver's tool can cut equally left or right or up or down. The engraver can use very fine straight-edged cutting tools unlike the V-shaped knives and chisels used by linoleum and woodcut makers. There are two other characteristics not found in either linoleum or side-grain wood (woodcut wood): control of the cutting line and great durability.

The grain of the wood actually helps to hold and control the engraving tool so that a rapport develops between engraver and block. As the point of the tool descends below wood surface, the block seems to push back and at the same time to grip the point firmly, keeping it steady during the cutting of the line. In a pen or pencil drawing the line is dependent upon the steadiness of the hand making it; the paper offers no resistance. In an engraving, once the tool descends into the wood, the point is held in a groove and even a shaky hand or arm can make quite a steady line.

The other important characteristic of end-grain wood is its great durability. When the block is in the press, the millions of grain ends push back against the pressure exerted by printing, and offer so much resistance to being smashed down by the press that a wood-engraving block can be used in any kind of letterpress printing press and will produce hundreds of thousands of impressions, each one identical in all respects to the first one. In the 1770s Thomas Bewick made a wood-engraving masthead for a newspaper that remained sound after more than a million impressions.

Engravers have tried many other materials, but neither metals (which raise burrs and dull tools very quickly) nor plastics (which chip out and are always either too hard or too soft) have been found useful. Only end-grain pieces of wood have the right qualities. They not only hold the tool firmly but also enable the point to navigate among the sides of the grains without causing either burrs or chip-outs.

Good boxwood will give sharp, clean lines, lighter in tone than the amber surface color of the wood, and as you cut each line, however short the stroke, you hear a pleasing "zip, zip, zip" sound as the tool creates the next part of the line.

By far the best boxwood was Turkish box, which came from the Crimea, and was used exclusively until the Second World War. Now, however, it has vanished from suppliers' lists. Some say it became extinct through overuse. I have heard that it is still available but must be imported in quantities too large for the limited needs of the engraver's boxwood manufacturer. Perhaps at some future time this superb wood will be reintroduced to a new generation of engravers.

Today boxwood quite suitable for all engraving purposes comes from South Africa or South America. Brazilian boxwood, the least expensive, is used as a student-grade wood in America, but it is very porous and its surface must be coated with a sealer-filler liquid, found in paint and hardware stores. New wood sealers can probably be used to make many other end-grain woods useful to the wood engraver, but very little experimentation has been done along these lines.

The wood requires years of preparation before it is suitable for engraving. First the small logs, some only three inches in diameter, must be thoroughly air dried, which means several years of storage in dry rooms. Then they are sliced into "rounds." In this rough state they are squared and glued together to make rows of blocks that are glued together. These rough slabs are put into a surface-finishing machine that grinds off most of the roughness from both sides. The final polished finish is given either by machine sanding (in America) or by hand planing and the use of a furniture scraper (in England). There is

Slabs of end-grain wood—maple and boxwood—in varying states of readiness for engraving. The white-coated blocks are prepared for photographic development.

much unavoidable waste in the processes. Wood is lost when rounds are squared before gluing, and the center of each round must be removed because of its relative softness. Blemishes—or places where a small limb grew from the tree—must be cut away as well. Of each round perhaps 40 percent ends up in a finished slab.

This painstaking manufacturing, which is mostly handwork, requires such diligence and skill that only a limited production of boxwood slabs is possible

from year to year. The rough rounds in their original state may be made usable, however, even with their softer middle sections and small imperfections left in. That would release much more wood for student use and lower the price as well. In addition, the student would experience the feeling of working on an actual piece of a tree. I have engraved on rough rounds for many years with great success. Good-sized cracks in the wood can be made acceptable by designing around them or by using them as part of the engraving. The boxwood slab is still the ideal, however.

The use of maple, pear, or cherry as engraving wood has long been the practice when lines do not need to be very fine. Maple, which is used for end-grain flooring and wooden pieces of type, can be quite satisfactory and is easily obtainable. Modern machinery and electronic gluing are only two of the new technological improvements that may produce new engraver's wood by the yard instead of by the inch. I have found excellent maple slabs, with many small blocks glued together into large sizes, and because they are smoothly finished on both sides, two working surfaces are available for the price of one.

The grain of engraver's wood runs from the underside of the slab to the working surface, and moisture will enter and leave the wood by this same route. A large slab of end-grain wood placed over a saucer of water absorbs moisture from the air near the saucer, causing the grain to swell. In a few hours the slab will no longer be flat, but will look like a square section from a wooden balloon. As much as an inch of difference may exist between the corners of the slab and its center. If this happens, the wood can be returned to its original flat condition by turn-

A round of boxwood. The imperfections make it necessary to cut out only the best pieces and glue them together into a single perfect block.

ing it over and letting the other surface absorb moisture until the block flattens out. Moisture will affect all blocks, large and small. For that reason end-grain blocks, whether fresh from the woodmaker or completely engraved and aged many years, are stored vertically, with a slight air space between each block, on shelves well away from changes in moisture. New slabs should be stored in their newspaper wrappings until needed. Vertical storage assures that moisture will penetrate both surfaces equally, preventing the possibility of warpage.

The glue traditionally used to join the blocks together is *not waterproof* and is quickly dissolved on the surface by spilled liquids, leaving hairline cracks where the glue once was (another reason for standing the block upright on your work table).

Caution also applies to temperature changes. All woods are affected by sudden changes in temperature, and engraver's wood is no exception. Let the change be as gradual as possible. For example, never let direct sunlight fall on the surface of a block or within minutes it will crack, usually beyond repair. Even the heat of an incandescent light bulb too close to the block while one is engraving can cause warpage. Thomas Bewick's large "The Chillingham Bull" was left on a windowsill by an inebriated printer's helper and cracked irreparably in the sunlight. This story is often told as an admonition to new engravers.

A good rule is always to stand the block upright next to your engraving pad when you are not working. Not only will this prevent temperature or moisture problems, but also nothing can fall on the surface and make a dig or scratch. Wood-engraving tools are not the only things that will mark the sensitive surface of the wood. A sharp fingernail or sandpaper (except the very finest grade) will often scratch below surface. Anything solid dropped onto the block from a height of more than an inch or two will also damage it.

This does not mean that the wood surface is so sensitive that precautions approach surgical sterility, but it does mean that a healthy respect for the printing surface of the wood and the habits of holding it carefully in your hand and storing it properly when you are through will save many a despairing hour of wondering how that dent or scratch got there, and trying to remove it without affecting the lines that it crosses.

Minor imperfections in the surface can sometimes be removed by careful sanding or scraping. A wide wood chisel, say a half-inch to an inch in width, with its cutting edge absolutely straight (and perhaps the sharp corners gently ground to make them slightly round), can scrape down to fresh wood and remove surface scratches. The chisel is held vertically and pulled toward you so that it takes away very fine wood particles that are called "flour." Practice on another piece of wood first, for if you make a

A large slab of maple clearly showing the many smaller pieces glued together.

real hollow in the block, you will only have compounded your problem.

Large cracks can sometimes be filled with crack fillers, although this is seldom satisfactory because they often come out months later. A dent in the wood can sometimes be brought up to the surface by putting a drop of water into the dent and then moving a lighted match back and forth *over* the dent, turning the water to steam.

Large imperfections in the wood or errors made while engraving can be corrected only by removing that part of the surface and inserting a new piece of wood, but this is a delicate job best left to expert woodworkers. Commercially sold small round plugs that taper slightly can be tapped into perfectly round holes made by a drill press. A row of the plugs will actually correct a long crack, but the process is laborious and time consuming, and not for the amateur.

Sometimes you may want to alter a large section of a block or add on a piece of wood to make a larger engraving. A good woodworker can do this without too much difficulty, after a little practice. Boxwood slabs and blocks can be sawed on electric table saws if they are moved at a slow rate of speed against the circular blade or bandsaw blade. To plane the cut edge perfectly enough to join another piece of wood to it, however, requires the circular saw with planing bits inside it used by typesetters and printers for planing lead slugs. It's a lot simpler to join a piece of wood to your slab by holding it against the slab with a C-clamp, strong tape, or heavy rubber bands, and many an engraving has been made that way.

During your engraving career you may encounter these problems once or twice, but they are not to be considered part of the everyday mechanics of making a wood engraving.

Engraver's boxwood has been made these many years to the standards required for the commercial engravers at the turn of the century. The beautiful look of the wood—its height that of a piece of type, the perfection of the surface, and the very polish that feels good to the touch—these things come to us from another age. With the unwrapping of the block, the engraver experiences much the same joy that Michelangelo probably felt when he looked on the giant cubes of marble that were delivered by teams of horses to his studio. Let the wood be to you the same challenge the marble was to Michelangelo—a stranger that with diligence will become a friend. Despite the caveats expressed here, very few engravers have trouble with wood; and your engravings will not only be a delight to make, but, thanks to the virtues of the wood, will print as beautifully a hundred years from now as they will tomorrow. Bewick's blocks, many of them two centuries old, remain in the same state of perfection as the day he finished engraving them. It is an immortality of sorts, and it all begins with the block of wood.

3 The Engraving Tools

The wood-engraving tool is a beautiful instrument. Its solid steel shank and polished wood handle have been admired by many of my friends. The first time you try to use it, however, it will feel awkward and unable to answer to the hand; but, properly used, a sharp tool of the right size is capable of transmitting to the wood all the subtleties of hand and mind. There seems to be no limit to its sensitivity. Perhaps it is the very simplicity of the tool that makes it frustrating to use at first and extremely rewarding with more experience later on.

All the basic wood-engraving tools have the same profile from the side—a steel shank, a sharpened point, a curved belly, and a "tang" to which the wooden handle is affixed.

The beveled front surface of the tool is the only edge that is ever sharpened. The shank will gradually shorten over a lifetime of sharpening, but its cutting edge will perform until the shank has been entirely ground away, something that happens very rarely.

The shank is of unpainted and polished steel and is subject to damage by rust. Therefore it should always be kept very lightly oiled. Its cutting edge—along the bottom—must remain forever sharp, and the tool should be handled with care, never dropped, and never allowed to click against other tools. For this, and other reasons, engravers take great pains to keep their tools separated from each other. If one scoops them up and dumps them into a cigar box or a drawer willy-nilly, the cutting edges will inevitably become dented, even if only slightly, and the points may need resharpening. So the engraver uses a felt cloth with little pockets sewn into it, or a ribbon running through it which makes loops. The felts used for storing silverware are excellent, especially those used for spoons. Felt cloths of this type have the additional virtue of making it easy to pack your tools at the end of a session and put them away in the proper order, ready to be unrolled at a moment's notice.

Many wood engravings are made from start to finish with a single tool, but most engravers will want to have several tools, at least a half-dozen, and sometimes four times as many, acquired over the years.

Almost none of the tools sold for wood engraving today are true wood-engraving tools, no matter what it says on the box in the store or what the salesman in an art supply or hardware store may tell you. This even applies to wood-engraving kits made by well-known wood-engraving toolmakers.

The tools sold for wood engraving are only a few of the many tools manufactured by commercial firms. Most also make tools for jewelry engraving, metal engraving, and the finishing of photoengraving plates. The standards for these other trades were set seventy-five years ago, and the tool manufacturers continue in the practice of their forebears. I have often talked with the American and French manufacturers of these quasi-wood-engraving tools (there are none in England), and learned to my astonishment how little they know of the uses to which their tools are put. Several of them didn't even know the difference between wood- and photoengraving practice. Of the five tools sold in one American "wood-engraving set," not one was a true wood-engraving tool, and only one of them—a jewelry engraver's burin—could be used for engraving with any success.

We must establish the standards for ourselves and buy only those tools that actually work.

All commercially made wood-engraving tools, unless specially ordered, are manufactured an inch or more too long. The only explanation I can offer for this impossible length is that in the heyday of commercial engraving, when every wood engraver was a dedicated journeyman, the buyers liked to break off the ends of the shank themselves, to their own size. This does not make much sense, however, because it is easier to lengthen a tool that was made too short by affixing a longer handle. Handles came in many different lengths anyway. Commercial engravers had tools that after decades of use were only an inch or so long, with perhaps three-inch handles.

The common practice of an engraver who had just bought new tools was to put them in a vise, one at a time, with an inch or so of the point sticking up out of the vice jaws, then with a sudden sharp ham-

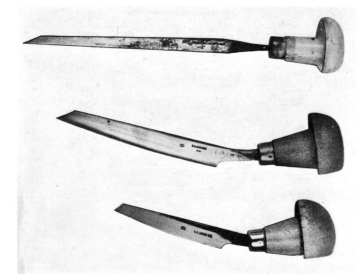

These tools have survived from the old days of engraving. From top to bottom: an unbelievably long tool typical of those once sold to engravers; an excellent splitsticker needing only an inch or so cracked off the front end; a tint tool of the proper length.

mer blow break off the tool just at the jaws. The laborious task of grinding down the fresh break into a bevel and then resharpening the tool had to be painstakingly performed on each tool. This procedure still applies today if the tool is too long.

The Proper Length of the Tool

The proper position of the *point* is just a little in front of the thumb when the tool is held correctly at the beginning of a stroke. The point can also be against the ball of the thumb, not sticking out. A slight movement of the wrist toward or away from the body directs the point ever so slightly, because the point is at the *fulcrum* of the thumb, at the place where the turning is made. If the tool is so long that the point sticks out an inch or more beyond the thumb, wrist movement of the slightest amount will move the tool a great deal.

When the handle of the tool is nestled in the back of your hand (see page 90) and the point is at the ball of your thumb, the tool is just the right length. If it happens to be too short, the handle can always be placed further inside the palm of the hand, so a shorter length of tool is really no problem.

Now that we have our standard for length, the next standard is the curve of the tool belly. Multiple liners (tools that make more than one line in a single stroke) do not need very much curve, although some

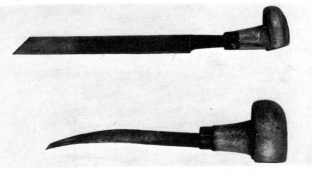

Photofinishing tools. The curved tool is used exclusively for making dots, while the other has a bottom edge too straight for wood engraving.

is desirable; but the angle and elliptic tint tools should have a curve almost as pronounced as that of a rocking chair rocker.

A wood-engraving tool differs from tools made for photoengravers' plate finishing because it has a convex belly throughout its entire length, while a photofinisher's tool starts with a concave curve and then either becomes flat or changes to a convex curve near the handle. By breaking off the concave front of the photofinisher's tool, you can adapt it for use in wood engraving.

The only flat tools used in wood engraving are the jeweler's diamond-shaped burins. These burins are so slight in cross section that if they were not straight they might buckle when you used them and bend out of shape.

The Three Basic Wood-Engraving Tools

Angle Tint, Elliptic Tint, and Multiple Liner

Despite the large number of lines found in wood engravings, virtually all engravings are made one line at a time. There are, however, two types of lines we can make, and the engraver quickly learns how to make both of them. One of these lines is similar to a line made with a ballpoint pen on paper. It is always

The three basic tools of wood engraving. From right to left: the elliptic tint or splitsticker, the angle tint or tint tool, and the multiple liner or shooter.

of equal thickness throughout its length, although it may curve or go straight. To make such a line we use a tool called the angle tint.

The angle tint is shaped in cross section like a wedge or a "V" with flat sides. When you engrave a line with an angle tint, the tool goes into the wood to a certain depth and then stays there throughout the entire cutting of the line. You can make it cut a slightly heavier line by pushing down on it somewhat, but to be used correctly it should only cut a line of single thickness. If you need a wider line, you must use a wider angle tint tool. Angle tints come in twelve different widths.

The elliptic tint tool also makes a single line; however, the line goes easily from thick to thin, or thin to thick. It is similar to lines made by the old-fashioned pen points that spread apart when pushed down on the paper. Unlike the angle tint, the elliptic tint has no fixed depth in the wood and can be pushed in a single stroke from a hairline to a broad line by changing the depth. Lifting the tool gradually out of the wood creates a line that becomes thinner and thinner. The curved belly dips and rises as it cuts the lines.

Elliptic tints come in twelve different widths, so a variety of line widths can be made easily. The engraver can also reenter the same line again and again to make it as deep—and therefore as wide—as he wants to. This technique is frequently used, but it

The lines in these engravings were made exclusively with angle tint tools of varying sizes. The width of the line hardly changes.

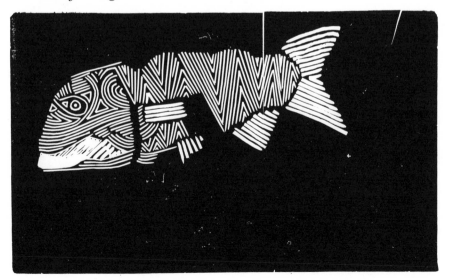

Engravings made with the elliptic tint tool. A single line thins and thickens along its course.

is best to have a range of tool sizes so that a wide line can be obtained in a single stroke.

While lines made by an angle tint seem to cross the area in front of our eyes without getting either closer to us or farther away, lines made by elliptic tints appear to come toward us or to recede as they get wider and narrow again. This is one of the main purposes of the elliptic tint. It is generally used for

engraving such things as portraits, in which the lines delicately trace the subtle features of an eye, a cheek, a nose.

The multiple liner is the third of the basic wood engraver's tools. It makes many lines in a single stroke and has two or more points, sometimes as many as twelve; however, five or six are usually sufficient. The multiple liner is called the "shooter" by engravers and is a very misunderstood tool. It appears to promise greater usefulness than a single tool, to say nothing of the time saved by being able to make five lines or so in a single stroke. But, unfortunately, after you make a stroke of five or six absolutely perfect lines, your second stroke of five or six lines next to it often will be made *imperfectly*. The result is seldom entirely satisfactory.

The shooter is one tool never dreamed of by Bewick. It was invented by toolmakers to clean out filled-in areas of the screened photoengraving metal

Engravings showing the multiple liner in action.

plates that came into popularity in the 1880s and are with us today. A good photoengraving finisher can take a shooter and drop it exactly into the matching lines of a copper or zinc photoengraving and "feel" the tool along until the lines have been cleaned. In wood engraving, where there are no already existing lines, the chances of a precise use of this tool are hardly possible.

But wait. There *are* lines in a wood engraving, too, which the shooter can feel. They are the lines made by the last stroke of the shooter. Suppose you were expert enough to overlap the next shooter stroke so that two of its five or six lines are actually in two of the grooves cut during the last stroke. If you could "feel" the previous lines well enough, you could cut three or four fresh lines exactly parallel and have a technique for covering a whole passage of the block with a very even set of lines. This is how commercial wood engravers used the shooter when they could not use ruling machines for one reason or another—for example, if the lines were curved slightly. With a little practice the shooter can make a beautiful mechanical set of lines, which engravers call a "tint" (more on that in Chapter 7).

Very few engravers need or use the multiple tool. Most students try one out in class, but spend their money on the single tools. However, some artistic engravers have used the multiple liner extremely

well. Its groups of lines can be made to show a certain charm. A very great novel, *Destiny* by Otto Nückel (1930), done entirely in wood engraving with no words, used the shooter as the only tool for nearly four hundred pictures.

Twenty-five years ago the multiple tool could be obtained in many grades. Fine shooters could cut three hundred lines per inch. Others cut one hundred fifty lines per inch to match the photoengraving screens used for magazine printing plates, or fifty-five lines per inch to match the plates used in newspaper printing. Some shooters were even as coarse as thirty lines per inch, or less.

In addition to the lines-per-inch measurements, the tools themselves had anywhere from two to twelve lines on each. A photoengraving finisher required nearly a hundred shooters, which meant a half-dozen or so in each screen. Many commercial wood engravers also had as many as a hundred shooters because their engravings were ruled so-many-lines-to-the-inch for use in newspapers and magazines.

Since the popularity of photoengraving has diminished with the growth of offset printing (which has no raised plates), the manufacturing of shooters has almost ceased. They are still made in a limited range of screens and points-per-tool, but very few are produced each year. A five- or six-line shooter in a screen of sixty-five lines per inch or coarser may prove useful to you. The finer shooters, which will make almost unreadable lines, are seldom used in printmaking or other artistic work.

The angle tint, elliptic tint, and multiple liner are the three basic tools. Throughout the text they will be called by their familiar names: tint, split-sticker, and shooter. All other tools are auxiliary and are seldom used for the actual engraving. Round and flat gravers (called "scorpers" in England) are small chisels of varying widths that are used primarily to remove from the block those areas that are not engraved but appear pure white in the finished proof. Some artistic engravers use these tools to make very broad lines or to provide special effects.

Sharpening the Tools

When the point of the wood-engraving tool is sharp, it cuts almost effortlessly in the wood, making a satisfying little sound as it cuts and turning the act of engraving into an act of joy. Actually, the cutting is done by both the tool's point and the whole section of the beveled front end that is submerged below the wood's surface. A sharp tool presents to the wood a perfectly flat-beveled facet with sharp shoulders whose edges cut the line cleanly.

Gradually, the shoulders wear away with use and the front bevel of the tool loses its flatness. Tools do

The Humfish. On one of Darwin's expeditions, some members carefully put parts of several insects together and as a joke presented the new "species" to Darwin asking him to identify it. "That," said Darwin, "is a humbug." And this is a humfish a student made using the three basic tools and combining their techniques.

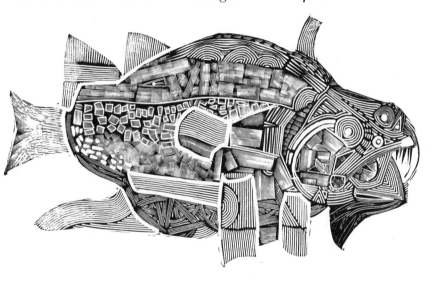

not become dull quickly, but when they do, they cease to respond properly. Often, cutting "just one or two more lines" will cause the tool to slip across the wood's surface, leaving a scratch.

It is a simple matter to lock a dull tool into a sharpening jig, place both jig and tool on a sharpening stone, give a few strokes back and forth on the stone, and then go back to work again. The principle of sharpening is simple. The tool must be placed upside down on an oilstone at exactly the angle of the bevel, which is the only part of the tool that is actually sharpened. In stroking the tool back and forth across the length of the stone, the old bevel is worn away to a new flat one with a sharp shoulder. The same method is used whether the tool is a tint, split-sticker, or shooter. The difficulty is in laying the tool on the stone and moving it without changing the angle or rocking the tool to the left or right. Old-time engravers, after years of practice, could keep the tool rigid as they sharpened by hand. It's a nice trick if you can do it.

A sharpening jig eliminates this problem. Though designed for different tools, a wood-chisel sharpening jig will hold the wood-engraving tools just as well. An English-made jig (see Appendix) is easily adapted and can be found in hardware specialty stores (see Appendix). This jig makes sharpening so simple that anyone can accomplish it the very first time. The jig opens and closes by turning a large screw, and if you line the narrowest part of the jaws with strips of sponge rubber (the kind sold in hardware stores for insulating door edges), they will hold the narrow shank of the wood-engraving tool perfectly. Once positioned, the jig is tightened with a coin in the slotted screw head and the tool becomes immobile.

The oilstone surface should be well oiled with an all purpose oil so that the little particles of steel float away in suspension from the surface of the stone and the pores of the stone are kept unclogged. The ideal stone size is two inches wide and six inches long. India or Arkansas Brand stones are excellent and are made with a coarse side for fast grinding and a fine side for the finishing strokes. The stones are usually packaged in wood or metal boxes and should be stored in these and kept covered against dust. The inside of wooden boxes should be shellacked

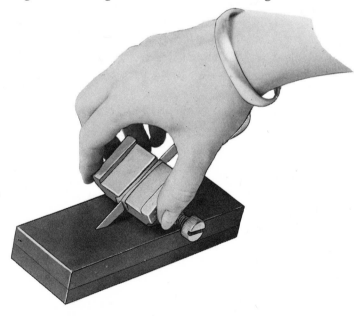

The sharpening jig.

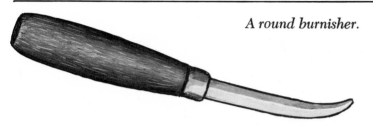

A round burnisher.

for protection against the oil, and even lined with a piece of felt or flannel to help float off the particles of steel. The stone and box should be kept absolutely flat when in use, and placed securely so that they are immobile during the sharpening process.

Sharpening will create a slight burr on the shoulders of the bevel and under the bottom of the point. This must be removed before the tool will cut properly. The shoulder burrs are removed by giving the tool a few strokes with a piece of very fine sandpaper called Crocus cloth that is sold in hardware stores. The burr at the very point of the tool is best removed by jabbing the point into a piece of soft pinewood a few times. Rub your thumb along the bottom edge of the tool to feel for the burr.

Finally, the standard engraver's test for sharpness is to push the point of the tool very gently across your thumbnail; if it "catches" on the surface, you can be sure it's sharp enough.

Unorthodox Tools

A tool frequently used by wood engravers to darken a passage of lines or tint that has gotten too light is the *burnisher*. It is not used for actual engraving but is pressed down on the tops of the lines to smash them slightly, producing a wider black line and leaving less white in between. Both flat and round burnishers are readily available. The burnisher can also be used for rubbing a proof from an inked block.

Jewelers' burins are designed to engrave names and designs on trophies, bracelets, and rings, but can also be used to engrave in wood with certain effectiveness. Leonard Baskin uses them almost exclusively for his impressive engravings. The burin is a diamond- or square-shaped piece of tool steel that is ground and sharpened at a bevel on the engraving end and pointed upward to form a tang at the other, to which a handle is attached. The burin shank is flat across its entire length to make it as rigid as possible. The cross section is often very tiny compared to that of a tint tool. Burins are good for cutting the square-, diamond-, or lozenge-shaped areas made by intersecting black pen-and-ink lines in certain kinds of ink drawings on the wood block.

Miscellaneous hand tools. Any kind of object that will mark the surface of the woodblock may be considered a wood-engraving tool. For example, the punch, used to make square or rectangular holes in wood for plugging, is a tool of sorts. So is a plain nail, tapped again and again by a hammer to make tiny holes. The hammer itself could be considered a tool for making dents. In skilled hands the handsaw can

An engraving made quickly with the vibrating engraving tool.

An electric vibrating engraving tool.

An engraving made by pounding nails into the surface of the block.

produce certain kinds of lines not easily obtainable otherwise.

Remember, a wood engraving is not an end in itself but rather a means of making exciting pictures. Anything you use that makes that possible is therefore a legitimate tool for working on the wood. I do not mean to suggest that present tools are not satisfactory or sufficient, but new ideas may require new tools to supplement the old ones. The creative engraver will not let tradition prevent further visual discoveries from taking place on the woodblock.

One new tool undreamed of by nineteenth-century engravers is *the electric vibrating engraver* sold in hardware stores to "write on glass and metal." This mechanism has a carbide tip that makes several thousand thrusts a minute. When rapidly stroked across a woodblock, it makes a dotted line, and, used as the only tool, it can make a simple wood engraving in approximately ten seconds. Traditional engravers may be appalled by this suggestion but the vibrating engraver can quickly introduce a classroom of very young students to engraving without anyone getting hurt using the regular tools. In a few minutes everyone can finish a block and proceed with the steps of inking, proofing, and comparing. The vibrating engraver requires very free and quick strokes of the hand. It has its own aesthetic, and its potential as a creative wood-engraving tool is great.

Indian head engraved by Leonard Baskin using a burin.

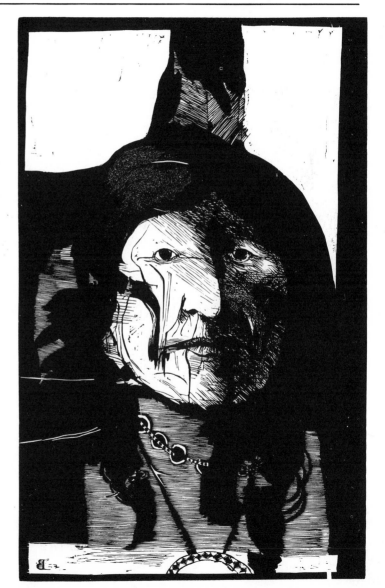

An engraver at the routing machine.

The creative router. Another electric tool with which remarkable experimental pictures have been made is the router. Designed to remove unengraved wood very quickly, the routing machine comes with a variety of bit widths and can make thin or thick lines at great speed and under perfect control. The large floor-mounted routing machines used by photoengraving shops cost many hundreds of dollars but used ones can often be found for a fraction of their original cost. Not many engravers have the necessary floor space or can afford the expense. Printmaking departments in schools and wood-engraving societies that collectively own proofing presses, however, may find the routing machine a valuable and creative asset. Small portable electric routers used by carpenters to cut hinge cutouts in doors will also work well in the end-grain wood if the bits are not so wide they prevent proper control of the instrument.

The "rollette." This is a steel wheel on a handle with a crisscross design that can be rolled across the wood surface to produce interesting textures and perhaps even entire drawings. It is made by engrav-

ers' toolmakers and can sometimes be found in photoengravers' and printers' supply houses.

As an engraver, you will want to examine the full range of tools and the techniques they make possible. There are punches with letters, numbers, circles, or symbols; little electric motor-driven carving tools that are held in the hand or used at the end of a flexible shaft—and many others. New technology will create even more tools, and new visual statements made on the woodblock may well come from a discriminating use of these unorthodox but valid new tools.

Picture engraved with the router.

4 Other Equipment

Inks

Anyone who has made a "potato print" in kindergarten will remember that half of a raw potato with a design cut into it is dipped in some smeary kind of ink and then pushed again and again onto a sheet of paper in a primitive step-and-repeat pattern. The loose-flowing ink is easily transmitted to the paper by the pressure of the hand on the potato. In a manner of speaking, the arm is the printing press and furnishes all the pressure needed.

The linoleum block is usually the next form of printing to be tried. Again a picture is cut into the block, and liquidy ink squeezed out of a tube is smeared on the block with a hard roller. Some of my sixth- and seventh-grade colleagues made proofs by laying the paper on the floor, placing the block on it upside down, and stamping as hard as they could on the back of the block. Other, less rambunctious students used a light metal "press" made for the purpose that could be brought down onto the block and paper hard enough so that the moist thick ink could make its soft transfer. Ink often pushed into the white spaces where it was not wanted.

Wood engraving, however, requires different inks and paper and a much sturdier press. A wood engraving becomes a printing plate the moment it is completed. It is identical in kind to every other printing plate used on letterpress printing presses. It must print so that none of the lines fill with ink and all the inked wood prints perfectly black. Proofs are judged on the excellence of the idea and execution of the illustration. The paper and ink must remain unobtrusive to allow emphasis on the work on the block.

A stiff proofing ink used by printers is preferred. Proofing ink (sometimes called proving ink) is unique to letterpress printing. Unlike the printing inks of both letterpress and offset printing, it contains little or no drier and lasts longer in the can, and on the inking slab. I have seen proof presses in the back of letterpress shops where the ink has never been cleaned off the inking slab, but just used up and more ink added from day to day.

Most proofing inks come in several grades, according to the amount of grinding done in their manufacture. The very finest inks are those that have been most meticulously ground. The wood engraver should choose a more expensive grade because the results will be far superior. A pound can of ink will probably last for two to ten years in the studio of a single engraver, making the slight additional cost well worth it.

Proofing ink is odorless, very stiff, and jet black. It will remain "wet" on the slab for many days. Printing inks undergo a chemical change as they harden, and as a result cannot be dissolved with thinner. On the other hand, proofing ink is always soluble and will easily wash off the roller and slab at the end of a week. If you cover the slab with paper to keep the dust off, it will always be ready for use.

If you plan to use colors, you will need printing inks, which have almost the same qualities except that they will dry out faster and must be cleaned from roller and slab after every session. In selecting printing inks, it makes no difference whether they are for letterpress or offset.

The proper way to get ink out of the can is to scrape off only the surface layer of ink with a flexible putty or pallette knife, leaving a new but flat surface underneath. Digging little holes with the corners of the putty knife creates a greater surface exposed to air, which hardens the ink and makes its removal from the can more difficult the next time.

The ideal solvent is odorless, fireproof, chemically safe when inhaled or touched, and harmless to rubber rollers. When wiped from work areas, it should not stain or leave a film of oil, but it must be strong enough to dissolve proofing inks and old dried inks quickly. No solvent like this exists, and we are at the mercy of whatever the printing supply house can furnish. All solvents must be handled with care; follow the advice and warnings on the label. Solvents are highly potent industrial chemicals and must be treated as such, used in adequate ventilation, avoiding contact with skin. Rags soaked with solvent should be stored in metal containers to prevent fire.

Neither paint thinner, turpentine, or kerosene can replace printer's solvent. The last two leave a slight residue of oil that is not easily removed and inhibits the proper clinging of ink to the block and paper.

Never pour solvent directly onto the wood-engraving block or wipe a solvent-soaked rag across the surface. While it may not actually harm the block, it will stain the entire visible surface—both lines and top—and destroy the aesthetic beauty of the wood itself.

To remove the excess ink from the block before it is stored, simply take several proofs on newsprint paper without reinking. This "blind" proofing keeps the ink from drying and forming a layer above the wood. As dried ink builds higher and higher, such a surface becomes quite different from the original engraving below. Blind proofing is usually enough to remove nearly all the ink, but a final cleaning can be given with a soft rubber eraser, free of grit. Pink Pearl erasers, known to every American schoolchild, are ideal for this purpose and will even remove caked (but not dried) ink from the block. Do not

erase near the ink slab or you will spoil it with eraser rubbings.

To ink the block, you will also need a slab not quite as high as the wood and a soft rubber or plastic roller (often called a brayer). An ideal slab is smooth and impermeable to both ink and solvent—plate glass with a half-inch of paper underneath, a piece of plywood covered with formica, marble, plastic, or sheet metal. If you lack studio space, a portable slab is best, but if you do have the room, make a permanent slab by screwing wooden strips into the tabletop on three sides to hold the slab firmly in place. The fourth side, of course, is that against which the block will be placed.

Inking rollers are made of rubber or plastic that is soft enough to be temporarily dimpled if you push into it with your finger. The hard rubber rollers used in block printing or photographic ferrotype tinning are unsuitable for engraving. Beware of certain "composition" rollers made to this day with molasses and glue. They will give you all sorts of trouble—melting in hot weather, hanging in grotesque festoons on the roller core. The handles of most rollers are designed to keep the roller raised slightly above the table or slab so that the rubber or plastic will not flatten when the roller is stored.

Proofing equipment: an ink slab, brayer, and proofing press. Taped across the bed is a board with register pins on it.

A wide roller is best, although it may be expensive. The preferred size is six or eight inches, but four inches will suffice. If your engravings are going to be very large, you will do well with a ten inch roller, which is heavy and takes a strong arm to handle. Soft four-inch or four-and-one-half-inch rollers with a diameter of more than an inch are commonly found in art supply stores and are very good.

Paper

Wood engravings are proofed on papers identical to those used for letterpress or offset printing. The best

An inking roller or brayer.

ones are smooth papers used to print newspapers, books, catalogues, and magazines. The hardness of their surface takes the proofing inks perfectly and preserves intact all the fine lines of the engraving. The thick, rough construction papers of linoleum blocks and side-grain woodcut printing and the hand-made papers from Japan and elsewhere are useless for our purposes.

The cheapest paper is smooth newsprint, which is available in only one color—a light oatmeal gray. The rough-grade newsprint sold for sketching should not be used. The beauty of proofs on newsprint is seldom surpassed by even the most expensive coated stocks. It is also good for overlays and removing ink from blocks. Its low cost makes it ideal for students. Newsprint's fatal drawback is that it yellows and grows brittle with age and exposure to air. After a few years it will crack at the slightest touch. Therefore, while you may have plenty of proofs on newsprint, use other, more permanent papers as well.

Not all printing papers are good for proofing wood engravings. "Bond" paper and various uncoated letterpress and offset papers give poor results. Certain heavily "calendered" uncoated papers, however, are excellent. Calendering is a method of making uncoated paper smoother by running it between smooth steel rollers during the manufacturing process. Sample several papers if you can. One kind may give a rich black proof, while another, almost identical variety will give an uninteresting grayish proof.

Most of the papers used for etching and lithography are in this category of uncoated papers and are too heavy and expensive.

If wood engravings are made for reproduction, to obtain the cleanest, sharpest black against white proof, some kind of enameled paper is ideal. There are many brands, but all of them have been coated, while wet, with earth or clay on one or both sides and then run through steel rollers to give them a finish ranging from eggshell to gloss. Enameled paper comes in white and shades of tan, buff, and pastel and is sold by the paper houses that supply printers. Seventy-pound offset enamel is a fairly heavy paper, and sixty-pound a bit lighter weight. All printers'-paper houses have sample swatch books on hand, and you can feel the different thicknesses of paper and decide which one suits you best. They can also furnish you with samples. Paper houses usually sell in large volume, and you can save money by buying collectively with a group of your wood-engraving friends. This also helps to cut the cost per sheet, which is high when you purchase only a few sheets. For good customers, many paper houses will even cut the large sheets into smaller sizes, although some charge for this extra service.

Two Additional Kinds of Paper
Super-enamel and Tissue
Super-enamel paper is not only coated but is cast like glass instead of being run through rollers. This

cast-coated paper is extremely smooth and shiny and very impressive when used for proofs. It is also expensive, but the cost can be cut down by ordering it coated on one side only. Kromekote, a brand name super-enamel paper, gives a fine professional look to proofs, superior to most enamel papers. It is ideal for "scratching" a proof to see what wood should be removed next. The coating on Kromekote is impervious to ink, which must dry on the paper surface because it cannot soak in. Proofing inks, which take a long time to dry, will smear for weeks or months if you handle the proof improperly.

Tissue refers to a variety of special papers. Some Japanese tissues work beautifully with wood engravings, but most of the samples I have tried do not give the rewarding richness of jet black against white. The very uneven thickness of handmade tissues can cause part to be light in one proof and then darker in the next. Troya, an American machine-made brand-name paper, is quite suitable in all respects for proofing wood engravings. It is expensive but very beautiful.

Another "arty" paper, called Tyvek, has fibers that show through to give a very opulent look. Technically, it is not really paper at all, but a plastic cloth cut and sold like paper. It takes ink beautifully and, like Troya, gives prints of museum quality.

Actually, these "expensive" papers—Kromekote, Troya, Tyvek, and others—only cost a few cents more per sheet and are exciting to experiment with.

Presses

A wood-engraving block can be inked and proofed thousands of times. Engravers sign and number the proofs they sell, exhibit, swap, or give away. Much experimental work can also be done with a block

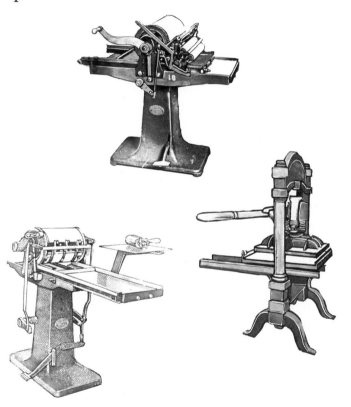

Several of the old proofing presses that can sometimes be found today.

during proofing (this is described in Chapters 9 and 10).

The rewards of proofing are greatest if you have the proper kind of proofing press; however, anything that presses is a press. Without pushing very hard, your thumb, pressed down on a sheet of paper that covers an inked block, will proof a small wood engraving of one-half inch by one-half inch. Most blocks will be much larger, but if that same pressure could be repeated on every half-inch of the larger block, a perfect proof would be obtained. Since this is neither practical nor possible, we use a press that mechanically pushes hard enough to squeeze the block and paper together. There is nothing mysterious or complicated about it.

Book presses, those iron tabletop models often displayed in stationery stores, make poor presses for wood engraving because the pressure will not be even unless the block is perfectly centered under the plate. A good proof of a small block can be obtained, but much love and understanding is required.

Wood-engraving proofs are best made on a good, sturdy press that is capable of enough pressure—rarely needed—to proof a large block without danger of breaking. The two kinds of proofing presses in use today—platen and cylinder—have remained unchanged for over a hundred years.

The platen press pushes a flat cast-iron plate against the block all at once. Thomas Bewick, Benjamin Franklin, and generations of printers and engravers used this kind of press. Early models were made of wood, but in the 1820s wood gave way to cast iron. Washington, Albion, and Columbian brand presses are typical of this kind. They are nearly all represented in museums, although occasionally a Washington press turns up on the market. Today a small one is worth more than a thousand dollars, while Albions and Columbians run from two thousand to five thousand dollars. Yet there are perhaps a dozen Washingtons in the basements of printing equipment companies, rusting to death and yours for the asking.

The cylinder press is the most common proof press today. It consists of a cast-iron bed over which a cast-iron or steel cylinder rides, permanently fixed at about one inch above the bed. Tiny hobby models, with cylinders one inch in diameter, are unsuitable for engraving. Larger models, used for proofing type galleys, have hard rubber rollers on iron cores and are quite useful for wood engraving. Their cylinders range from two and one-half to three and one-half inches in diameter and have a handle by which they are pulled across the bed.

Any one of the larger cylinder presses makes an ideal wood-engraving press. It can proof entire pages or large plates of metal or wood. Some of these presses are floor models with cast-iron cylinders ranging from six to twelve inches in diameter. Vandercook models Nos. o and 1 are perhaps the handiest, but many others are just as good. They can be found in letterpress printing shops, at printing auctions, and, in limited supply, in the "junk" sections of printers' machinery houses. If you bargain well, you can buy one for fifty dollars, but prices usually run to several hundred dollars. Of course, when new, they cost a great deal more.

In all but rare cases the proofing presses that require separate inking are best for making single impressions. Only with considerable effort over several hours can you make an edition of a hundred black-and-white prints. However, a letterpress *printing* press, once set up for production, can turn out an edition of a hundred prints in about ten or fifteen minutes, with the printer feeding in the paper, one sheet at a time, while an electric motor or a foot treadle turns the massive machinery. Of course, such a press can be used for proofing individual blocks, but it is difficult and time consuming to set up because the beds of these presses are almost always vertical and the block must be locked in place so that it cannot fall out.

Small hand-operated printing presses can be quite satisfactory for proofing and printing wood engravings. In England the Adana Company makes one, and the Kelsey Company offers one in the United States. Neither one will proof as fast as a printing press, but both are adequate and will turn

out an edition in no time at all. Also, the inking is automatic. The main drawback is the limited range of sizes. The largest model can only handle blocks of six by eight inches or less. New, these presses cost several hundred dollars each.

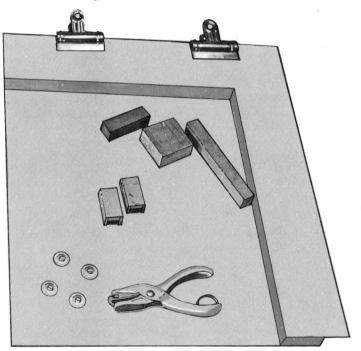

A simple handmade proofing jig: two spring clips to hold the paper in place, several pieces of wood (called "furniture") to position the block, two magnets to secure the block to the iron bed, register pins, and a paper punch.

Proofs can also be made on etching presses, which are normally used to apply great pressure to thin metal plates. Most of them are adjustable, however, so the gap between bed and roller can be greatly increased. Excellent proofs can be obtained, but since these presses have the power to smash down wood-engraving lines more easily than proofing presses, must be used with care.

Proofing without a Press

If you push only by hand on one small part of the block at a time, even the largest block can be proofed without any mechanical help at all. This can be accomplished by rubbing a spoon briskly and firmly over the block. With a *proofing jig* to hold the block firmly in position, you can obtain very professional results. A simple jig is inexpensive to make (see Appendix).

The jig consists of a flat piece of smooth iron, which will be the bed of the "press," and two iron strips mounted on narrower strips of wood so that the iron strip hangs over the outside edge. Two powerful magnets and several small pieces of wood "furniture" position and secure the block. The paper is held firmly in place on the metal ledges with either spring clips or register pins. A paper punch will make the necessary holes in your proofing paper so that it can be slipped over the pins. A burnisher or spoon achieves the actual proofing with superb results (see page 117). Obviously, you can easily make your own proofing jig, or you can order one ready made (see Appendix).

5 The Studio: Setting Up a Work Place

Wood engravings have been made in waiting rooms, dentists' offices, on the upper deck of buses, grassy slopes outdoors, and many other unlikely places. All that is actually required is a tool easily carried in one pocket and a block in another. Students in my classes have worked sprawled on the floor, curled up in corners, elbow to elbow at crowded tables. They don't seem to need a straight-backed chair, or even a chair at all; nor do they seem to mind bending their necks and backs far over their work, or working almost without light.

These practices would never suit the old-time engravers, or anyone who plans to work steadily for a long period of time. Even though my father made some of his most beautiful engravings at a rickety card table, I strongly suggest that you work on a sturdy table or desk with a wobble-free chair.

The proper engraver first sits bolt upright in a chair and then relaxes enough so that the arms hang freely at the sides and the neck tilts forward slightly, but not much. The block should rest on some device or a pile of books at a level about six to eight inches from the eyes.

The light in which you work should be strong but not glaring. Engravers need the same kind of

A nineteenth-century wood engraver at work.

light required by tailors, industrial miniature parts assemblers, and architectural draftsmen. A lot of lumens should be available at all times, not over the entire room, but in the immediate area of the block.

Thomas Bewick often engraved by the light of an oil lamp that was concentrated into a single beam by a water-filled glass globe made for that purpose. The commercial engravers in my father's shop preferred to sit near the windows, but they kept the black shades pulled most of the way down all day. Gooseneck lamps with sixty-watt bulbs, which burned their hands and sometimes damaged the blocks, provided lots of light for them. Blue "daylight" incandescent bulbs were used, but when fluorescent fixtures were invented, almost every engraver in the shop switched to the long two-tube lamps that were clamped to the back of the desks. They provided steady, plentiful light, bluish in color and cool to the touch. Because the tubes were a foot or more long, they cast no direct shadow. Today, the fluorescent lamps that come in circles around magnifying lenses are ideal. The regular two-tube lamps used by stenographers and draftsmen are also good.

Chairs that have straight backs and adjustable rests for the small of the back are ideal. There should be no arm rests because engravers' arms must move freely while at work and not rest on chair arms or tabletop.

The block, which should be about six inches from the eyes, is best engraved when it is slanted toward the engraver, nearly parallel to the engraver's face. The support surface on which the block rests should be smooth, assuring the easy, frequent pivoting of the block clockwise or counterclockwise without causing a curved line to waver as it is being engraved.

A sand-filled leather pad is traditional for this purpose, but these days they are somewhat hard to find. They can be made from a large piece of leather cut into circles. These are wet and stretched smooth

A student in one of my classes just getting started. The block rests on a sand-filled leather pad which is supported by a stack of cork rounds glued together. The tools are kept safely within reach in a tightly rolled piece of corrugated paper.

side out over convex plastic forms. They are then sewed by a shoemaker, leaving a small opening for filling each bag with sand. The last step is sewing or gluing the opening. These pads, which are not very expensive if you make a batch of them, are entirely suitable for wood-engraving purposes. They can also be purchased (see Appendix).

Linoleum also makes a smooth surface for the block. An inexpensive support can be made by anyone handy with wood. If the support has a lip on the front that hangs over the edge of the table, it offers greater stability. These supports are ideal for classroom situations where students can get them out easily and transform an otherwise flat table into an excellent place to engrave.

Once your table is set up, there is the question of a magnifier of some sort. Is this necessary? Almost all the high school and college students I work with never use a magnifier of any kind, and the young apprentices hired to learn commercial engraving in the old days seldom used any kind of magnification except for the smallest details. The rule seems to be that if you need a magnifier, use it. Obviously, you must see the work your tool is doing in the wood. If your particular style calls for absolute exactness, then magnification of some kind can be a big help. One way or another, you must be able to see the point of the tool clearly in the wood, the exact place that it is cutting, and the line that it is making. Much of the

The support for the leather pad.

amazement of visitors who examine the minute details in your blocks would vanish if they used a pair of magnifying binoculars, a large single-lens convex glass, or one of those industrial-type assembly lights that combines magnification with fluorescent light. Any one of these can be the engraver's most helpful accessory.

If you are going to get a magnifying headpiece (which can be used with eyeglasses, by the way), choose one that can be pushed up out of the way when you are not using it and which focuses about

A twentieth-century commercial engraver in my father's shop. He is wearing a set of magnifying goggles, which many engravers prefer to a magnifying glass on a stand. Ruling machine is in right foreground.

six to eight inches in front of your eyes. Any other distance is either so near that your hands are almost against your magnifier, or so far that you are not really getting all the benefits of the magnification. A No. 5 Magnifocuser, sold in the United States, is just about right.

Old-time wood engravers used a jeweler's loupe or similar small single lens that was attached to a stand. These could only be used with one eye, which placed a severe strain on both eyes—one by remaining closed and the other by fine focusing for long periods. This practice is not at all recommended. Sometimes, for extremely fine detail, undoubtedly much finer than needed by today's artists and printmakers, the engraver placed a high-power "linen tester" glass directly on the block, which gave supermagnification. If you are doing tiny lettering, or other high detail, you may want to use this kind of magnification, but only for very limited viewing periods, and only with one eye.

There is no eyestrain in normal wood engraving. In fact, there is no strain of any kind when wood engraving is properly done. If your tools are sharp, your hand will push them easily across the wood almost effortlessly. If the light is strong, your eyes will easily see what you are doing without staring or tension. If your chair is comfortable and helps to support your back, your entire body will stay relaxed.

Like other creative acts, wood engraving must be done in a kind of mental privacy so you can concentrate without the distractions of television, the ringing of the telephone, or noises from the street or the apartment next door. Once you have conceived a subject and have a "feeling" about how you are going to engrave it, you plunge yourself into a kind of creative trance that can take you uninterruptedly from start to finish. This does not mean that you have to finish a wood engraving in one sitting, but only that each "sitting" should be as free from interruption as possible. If you must pause, for any reason, it will take a few moments or more to resume your work and to remember what you are doing, thinking, and planning as your next steps on the block.

Obvious as they may sound, there are a few good rules to follow for making the act of wood engraving as continuous as possible. Wear old clothes so that you don't have to worry about getting chalk or ink or dirt on them. A smock or an apron is fine. Work on an old desk or table that you don't mind cluttering or scratching. Be as unself-conscious as possible. It is best to work where spouses and children are not going to pass by and glance at what you are doing. A desk in the living room is probably out. There will be time enough to show your work when you are ready, not before. Even a well-meant comment on the merits of an engraving not yet ready to be shown can stop you dead in your tracks. Have your tools sharp before you begin so you don't have to stop to sharpen them in the middle of your work. If you have to look for the stone, oil, or sharpening jig, you may decide to get a beer or soda out of the icebox, and very soon your concentration will fade away.

It's fine to eat, drink, or smoke while you are working as long as your concentration stays on what you are doing. If the enthusiasm with which you started the engraving can be maintained throughout, the result will be superb. It is the transmission of

The engraver's workplace. (From a German printing magazine of the 1920s.)

enthusiasm that makes an engraving come alive. The viewer will see your intensity and excitement in the finished picture. Without that excitement, your engraving, however technically perfect, will remain somewhat lifeless. Last of all, let it be said that there is nothing wrong with wanting to make something beautiful and to have people like it. The very sensitivity that makes you, like everyone else, seek approbation helps you to do good work. These two sensitivities are really one, and neither is anything to be ashamed of.

Basements make ideal working areas. They are private and casual. Also the additional equipment you may want—a printing press, inking area, and so forth—will require some space. If you have to sacrifice the daylight window of an upstairs room for the sanctuary of a basement, choose the basement. In the final stages of the engraving you will probably need to shuttle back and forth from the engraving bench to the press many times, and they should be as close together as possible.

Not everyone has an abundance of space. Some will be able to use the printmaking workshops in high schools and colleges. In many ways these are ideal because they offer a variety of presses and a chance to learn from the work of other students. Other novices may find adult printmaking workshops that offer the same advantages. Today most of them have proofing presses, although they are used principally for linoleum or wood-block printing.

If you are enterprising and committed, you may be able to form a wood-engraving club whose members share the expenses of proper presses, papers, inks, and other equipment. The wood-engraving club also provides a stimulating atmosphere in which members may discuss historical antecedents and current happenings, or may acquire memorabilia and trade proofs with one another. A small members' gallery could exhibit the group's work. All sorts of other activities are possible—from field trips and competitions to monthly newsletters and lectures by invited guests.

The basement workshop of R. Hunter Middleton.

6 The Drawing: From Paper to Block

Direct Drawing on the Block

Some engravers draw directly on the raw woodblock without preparing the surface in any way.

Almost any medium will be suitable—pen, pencil, watercolor, or wash. Crayon or grease pencil will not do, however, because the grease forms a thick layer on the surface, and whatever is used must remain very thin. If you draw with a ballpoint or a sharp drafting pen, take care it does not depress or scratch the wood surface.

One advantage of direct drawing on raw wood is the speed with which it can be done. The engraving can be started while the impulse is still strong. The major disadvantage is that the raw wood surface is almost the same color as the wood underneath, which makes the lines hard to see as the engraving is made. This has not seemed to bother most students in my classes, however, indeed, many practicing engravers prefer this method over all others. If the engraver makes a simple drawing, its outline can be cut quickly and the block inked before the shading is begun.

Simple drawings can also be made on a block that has first been inked black at the proofing slab.

Remove the tackiness of the ink from the block by blind proofing on scrap newsprint.

Coating the Block

Chinese-White Methods. Many engravers coat the surface of the block with a whitening agent of some sort before the drawing is made. This added step is usually done very quickly with watercolor whites— the zinc and Chinese whites that come in cakes or tubes. The coating is laid on very thin, with the side of a soft watercolor brush, using as little water as possible.

The surface must never become any wetter than necessary, for water may dissolve the glue holding the pieces of the block together and create slight cracks, which, while not affecting the strength of the joint, damage the surface that we want most to protect.

Acrylic whites, or even light acrylic colors, can also be used to coat the block. While they must be mixed with water, once dry, they are completely waterproof.

Albumen Method. The most satisfactory of all possible coatings is made by sealing the surface with egg white and then covering the sealed block with an egg-white-and-zinc-oxide mixture that forms the final coat.

This method is a bit more difficult and time consuming than the simple application of watercolor whites, but it is most rewarding. It provides a sealed surface impervious to dampness on which any sort of drawing or photographic image may later be placed. Have a number of blocks ready to coat at one time so that you use up the entire mixture.

A mixture made from two large eggs will cover several hundred square inches or more and will probably be more than enough for you. Both the clear egg white and the zinc-oxide-and-egg-white solution will keep for a week in the icebox if their containers are completely sealed with foil and airtight.

Using powdered egg white instead of raw egg whites seems a good idea in theory but does not work in practice. In this case there is just no substitute for the raw egg.

Over a bowl, separate the white from the yolks. The yolks may be thrown away or eaten. (In our wood-engraving shop the yolks were always a special delicacy on coating days.) The whites of the eggs are beaten with a simple hand eggbeater until they become a homogeneous mass, with perhaps a slight froth on top. This clear liquid egg white is called albumen. Reserve half of it in a mortar or similar vessel for application later as the final white coat.

Now, set the raw woodblocks on the table. Dip

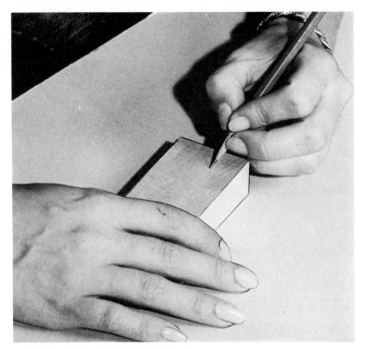

Drawing directly on the block.

your fingers into the albumen and rub it into the surface of each block, covering it evenly. Spread the albumen with your open palm, pushing from center to edge in all directions as you turn the block.

It will soak into the surface almost immediately. After the blocks have dried for a few minutes, apply a second coating, and again allow it to dry. Repeat this process until the blocks take on a shiny look and the egg white seems to remain on the surface rather

Coating the block in the traditional way:

separate the white from the yolk;

than soak in. It does not matter if the surface is slightly uneven. If you are in a hurry, all of these coatings can be put on in about ten minutes; if you are not, it is best to give the albumen a chance to dry thoroughly—about five minutes—between each coat.

The blocks now have a dark, glossy surface and may look almost good enough to eat. They are ready for a single coating of albumen-zinc-oxide solution. Powdered zinc oxide is sold in drugstores or chemist's shops and costs very little.

To make the solution, mix the reserved egg whites with a small amount of zinc-oxide powder. The powder resists mixing at first, but a mortar and pestle will make this task faster and easier. Add more powder in small amounts until the mixture becomes as stiff as a meringue. To test it, lift the pestle and let some drops fall back onto the surface. If they remain there, the solution is stiff enough. In the absence of a mortar and pestle, a teacup and a teaspoon will work well if you press the spoon against the sides of the cup until the powder and egg white have been thoroughly mixed. There should be no lumps, as these will spread unevenly on the blocks, causing

beat until frothy;

reserve half the beaten white;

difficulties later on.

To coat the blocks, place a dab from the spoon or pestle on the surface and spread it evenly with the open palm of one hand, pushing with the heel in rapid strokes. Hold the block with the other hand from underneath and revolve it in all directions.

If your first few blocks are not failures, consider yourself very lucky. The albumen-zinc-oxide solution, which is almost a paste, is not easy to spread evenly. It also tends to dry rapidly, leave a heavy layer in one place and a lighter one in others—and it streaks.

But after a few blocks, your two hands will co-ordinate much better, turning the block as you spread the solution. With just a little practice you will be able to control the even thinness of the layer much better. The best technique is to stop trying to spread the solution as soon as it begins to dry and, instead, to "polish" the block. This is done by "slapping" the block firmly with the same palm that you used for spreading, as you continue to rotate the block with the other hand.

The result of this process is a thin, even, slightly transparent white coating covering the surface of the

mix zinc oxide and reserved albumen;

test the consistency;

block. It will be very smooth to the touch and somewhat glossy in reflected light. The slapping seems to cause a glow to appear on the ultrasmooth coating.

If the coating is rough, spotty, or streaky, hold it under the faucet and dissolve it away, let the block dry, and start from the beginning again. Sometimes a drop of water on a heavy place will allow you to smooth it out, but the best way is always to put the entire coating on again.

Coating that is too thick may cause surface marks on the finished proof, or even flake off, leaving a small hollow. Sanding the surface with fine sand-

paper will often be sufficient to make it thin and even.

This hand-coating method works fine on the smallest blocks up to blocks about eight by eight inches. If you plan to coat many large slabs, first apply the clear white by rubbing with the palm as we did before, but then thin the albumen-zinc-oxide mixture with a little water and apply it with a very soft, wide sable brush. After it seems fairly even, lightly go over the drying coating with another dry sable brush, pushing harder and harder until the coating is dry and almost shiny.

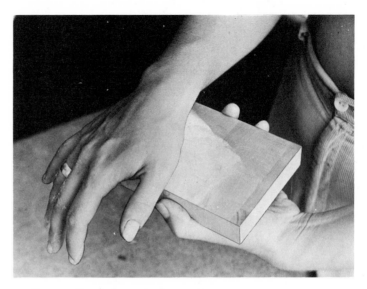

place a dab on the coated block;   *and spread evenly over the surface.*

Properly made, the albumen-zinc-oxide mixture makes an ideal, durable, all-purpose coating that lasts for the life of the block. It may be a lot of work for general use, but it is absolutely necessary for photographic image reproduction, which is discussed later.

The Purpose of the Drawing

There are two quite different interpretations of the purpose of a wood engraving, and each requires a different approach to the drawing. One holds that the engraving should be an exact reproduction of a finished drawing, while the other views the engraving as part of the creative process during which changes may develop in the drawing.

Those who view the woodblock as a mechanism for reproducing an already perfect drawing will tend to regard the act of engraving as a chore required to give "zip" to the drawing, and to convert it into printing-plate form. These practitioners will spend their creative energy on the drawing, whether directly on wood or on paper, completing the cross-hatching until they consider the work perfectly finished. At the completion of the drawing, all their interest may be drained and turning the drawing into a wood engraving then becomes a task almost without pleasure.

Drawings of this nature are often made with pens, so that every line is already in place. The engraver merely removes the wood that is not drawn upon.

This practice has been associated with wood engraving since the time of Thomas Bewick. He drew and engraved his own pictures; but even in his workshop someone gifted in drawing would draw fables or scenes on the blocks, while those with greater gifts in engraving did the actual cutting.

The art of engraving is no longer divided between designers and engravers. Someday that practice may be restored, but in the meantime every engraver is his own artist on wood. Even those who have made perfect renderings on the block should and most often do enjoy cutting them.

The other approach to wood engraving actually suits the medium better and can be much more exciting. The drawing is begun on the block in the rough and finished only by the actual act of engraving. The nature of an individual block and the tool you are using will influence the kinds of line structures you create. The excitement of letting the picture "happen" on the wood will give it a fresh quality and will hold the engraver's interest until the block is finished.

In this twentieth-century pencil sketch, opposite, the engraver has drawn high detail only where it will be needed—the eyes, nose, and mouth—and the rest of the drawing is roughly sketched in, showing only the position and shading. The engraver then interpreted his work into line structure, cutting dots, irregular lines, and other variations. When artist and engraver are the same person, it is the ideal practice—the one followed by Thomas Bewick in the eighteenth century.

Soft pencil, such as a No. 2B, can produce delicate and sharp outlines where needed, as well as make a soft, continuous shading without lines in which the relative tones are clearly indicated but the line structures are left to the engraving process. The lineless drawing technique works best for most people because it allows your interest in the engraving to increase as the work progresses, or at the very least, it sustains it.

Larry Rivers, the American artist, once made a statement that applies most appropriately to wood engraving. He said that the canvas of the artist is a rendezvous where what the artist knows meets the unknown. To the wood engraver this means that we bring all of our knowledge and skill to our rendezvous with the woodblock but also permit the unexpected to happen when we make our engraving. An unplanned, unanticipated development may make the engraving greater and more powerful, but we must be willing to risk failure as well. In any case,

the creative development of a soft drawing into a final engraving can be exceedingly gratifying.

A photographic image requires a decision—reproduce it exactly as the camera saw it, or treat it as a "soft drawing" and render it in terms of our own aesthetic instead of that of the camera?

Tone Drawings in Wash

A drawing in tones, instead of lines, can be made with certain gray paints used by photo retouchers. This kind of drawing forces the beginning engraver to decide before cutting what degree of gray will be in any given place.

Retouch grays come in black, white, and five or six tones graduating from light to dark. A four-tone drawing will include black, one dark and one light gray tone, and white. By being forced to articulate in advance where these tones will look best, the engraver has simplified his drawing, and has a firm idea of how it will be completed. This system takes much of the terror out of being confronted by a fully shaded drawing—even your own—and not knowing how to recreate it on the block. Later the engraver can work with a five- or six-tone drawing.

Keep the wash so thin on the wood surface that if you rub your finger over the block you can scarcely feel anything at all.

Tracing the Drawing onto the Wood

Tracing is another method of transferring a drawing onto the wood. Place the drawing in position over the wood with a piece of carbon paper, carbon side down, between drawing and block. Trace with a pencil or pen.

Remember, all drawings on the block are mirror images of the proofs they will make. If you are planning to trace your drawing, make it on semitransparent paper, and *turn the drawing over* when you place it on the block. This way it will trace in reverse and print correctly left to right when you proof it.

It is best to trace only the essential outlines and then put the tones on the wood with pencil or some other medium that will recreate on the wood all the qualities of your original drawing. Carbon paper knows no subtle tones, and you will find that the lights and darks of your original drawing will all seem dark if you trace them.

The Transfer Drawing

Pencil drawings on newsprint or offset paper can be transferred directly onto the coated block. If you used a coating that is not soluble in water, such as acrylic white or acrylic gesso, put a lather of soap on the block and place the soft pencil drawing on the lather. Now rub the back of the paper briskly with a spoon or burnisher to make the transfer. The entire drawing will actually be lifted off the paper and onto the wood surface in the correct reverse position. Some experimenting must be done in advance to make sure you are using the right kind of paper for the transfer, but once you have the idea, it will work well every time.

Transfers can also be made from other wood engravings, or from any kind of printing plate. Ink the plate or block and make a proof on a slightly heavy clear sheet of acetate. Then carefully place the wet acetate ink side down on a coated or uncoated block and burnish it until the ink has been transferred. This method is essential in making color plates and will be described in more detail later. It is also useful when you want to copy another engraving line for line, provided you have the original block at hand.

Protecting the Drawing on the Block

As you engrave over any kind of image, your fingers cannot help but smear the drawing. To protect it, lay a piece of thin paper over the block, creasing it at the edges. Now, remove the paper and tear or cut a window, exposing only the area you are going to engrave first. Then replace the paper and tape it down on the sides or bottom of the block. This way you can even proof the block as you work by inking only the open section (perhaps dabbing the ink on with your index fingertip instead of using a roller) and proofing the block with the protective paper in place. The paper should be very thin, to prevent its edges on the surface from printing as an indent in the wood.

The Photographic Image

Photography has been used to place images on the wood block since the time of the American Civil War. This method opens up a vast range of subjects to engrave—from a favorite snapshot to paintings, large drawings, lettering, and so on. It also simplifies working in color. The same negative may be printed on the number of blocks required, and you are ready to cut any one of the color blocks, without waiting for the key block (usually the black) to be completed (see Chapter 10).

Photography has the further virtue of making wood engraving more accessible to engravers who cannot draw well or who want to work with a subject on which the tone values have already been established.

The method itself is very simple. First you must have a photographic negative exactly the size that you plan to make your engraving. This can be obtained from any obliging friend who has a darkroom, or from a commercial photographer.

Choose or specify a film that produces a high degree of contrast, with plenty of middle tones. The ultra-high-contrast films used in offset lithography are excellent for this purpose if they are developed in a regular film or paper developer; the high-contrast developers eliminate middle tones and turn everything either black or white.

In addition to the same-size negative, you will need: silver nitrate crystals, hypo crystals (hypothiosulphate), distilled water, a five-by-seven-inch photographic tray, a hydrometer (to measure specific gravity), and a small glass cylinder to float the hydrometer in. All these supplies can be purchased in

High contrast photograph and . . .

. . . low contrast.

a photography store. Silver nitrate is rather expensive in small quantities, but a little goes a very long way. There are several prepared photographic emulsions on the market for various purposes, but none of them work with woodblocks, either because they

require too much water in the developing process or because they result in too much contrast.

The photographic emulsion is the light-sensitive layer of the film, plate, or, in this case, woodblock. To make this emulsion layer, stir a few crystals of

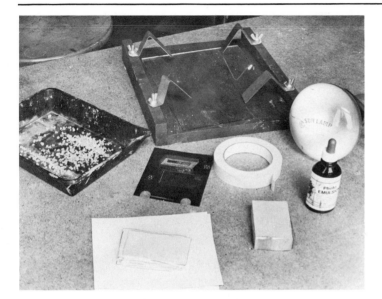

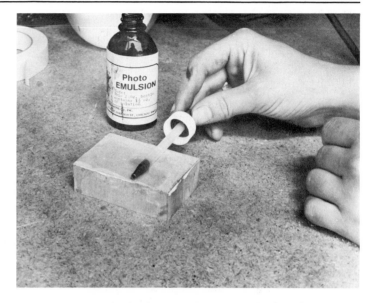

Equipment needed for developing on the block: sun-lamp, silver nitrate solution, masking tape, an albumen-coated block, high-contrast same-size negative, blotting paper, hypo crystals, developing tray, and a frame to hold the block.

Spreading the silver-nitrate solution on the block.

silver nitrate crystals into the distilled water in the small glass cylinder and take a reading with the hydrometer to determine the specific gravity. Add more crystals, a few at a time, until the reading stands at about 1040.

Silver nitrate solution is best stored in a brown bottle, marked "Poison" (which it is), and kept away from the light when not in use. On exposure to light,

the solution will stain anything it touches a deep, indelible brown. Be careful to keep it away from good clothing, and if you should spill any on your skin, wash it off with water immediately.

Once the solution is prepared, you are ready to sensitize the block. Subdued room light—daylight, incandescent, or fluorescent—will not cause any damage during the entire procedure. It is best to use a small medicine bottle with an eyedropper in the cap. Lay the block flat on a table, or, when you are more experienced, hold it with your hand underneath. Place a few drops of the silver nitrate solu-

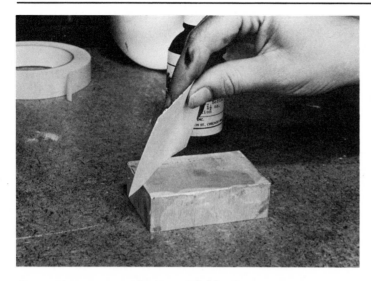

Removing excess solution with blotting paper.

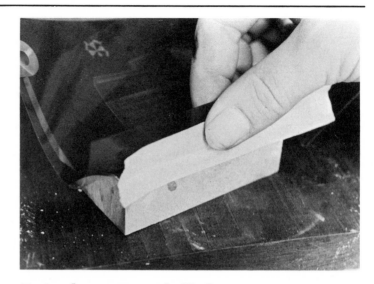

Taping the negative to the block.

tion on the albumen-coated block (Note: Acrylic coating does not absorb any of the emulsion). Spread them over the entire surface with the side of the eyedropper or similar device (a plastic straw is excellent). Allow the emulsion to dry, or wipe it off after a few seconds with a small piece of blotting paper—enough will have soaked into the surface to sensitize it. Blot up any drops that may have run down the sides. The block is now sensitized and ready for exposure.

Place the photographic negative against the sensitized block and tape it into position so that it can be lifted up and repositioned into exactly the same

place again. Because we want to reverse the image on the block, the shiny side of the negative should be against the wood instead of the dull side, as in normal contact printing.

Because the woodblock is nearly an inch thick, a printing frame cannot be used in the normal manner, but it can be adapted by setting aside the spring back of the frame temporarily and using rubber bands to press the block tightly against the glass. For our classes, we have duplicated the printing frame used by commercial engravers, as shown in the accompanying pictures.

The picture develops itself, as it exposes.

Securing it in the frame.

Making the exposure.

Exposure is made with an ordinary sunlamp bulb, or with any arc light that gives ultraviolet rays. Ultraviolet light of any kind is *very* harmful to the eyes and must never be viewed directly, so point the bulb away from you and others. Its reflection in the printing frame glass is not harmful at all, however; as a matter of fact, you should look at the frame during the exposure to see how dark the picture on the block is becoming.

With a sunlamp bulb at a distance of a foot or so from the glass, it will take about five minutes for the picture to develop, but you will see the wood darkening in the clear areas of the negative after the first minute or two. When the wood in the clear areas is quite dark, the print is ready, but if you are not sure, remove the frame from the light, keeping the bulb turned on, and lift up the taped negative to check. If you want a slightly darker picture, lay the negative down in *exactly* the same place and continue the exposure for another few minutes. If you turn the bulb off during the printing process, an internal safety device may prevent it from turning on again should you wish additional exposure time.

The print on the block should have almost the same quality as a regular drugstore photograph. It will continue to darken until it is totally black, however, unless the image is made permanent by "fixing" it in hypo. Any photographic hypo will do, but pure hypo crystals are very inexpensive and, when dissolved in water, do the job quite well.

Dissolve a small handful of hypo crystals in very shallow water in the photographic tray. Place the exposed block face down in the hypo-water for about thirty seconds, lifting slightly from time to time to make certain that the hypo fixes the image. Then run water gently over the fixed block for a few seconds to wash off the hypo, and lightly press the block's surface onto blotting paper or paper napkins to dry it. Take care not to touch the coated surface of the block while it is wet because it will smear. Once fixed and dried, the block is ready to engrave. The dried surface is permanent and will not smear or come off. If you are not pleased with the results, however, you can easily remove the image from the block while it is still wet and start over again.

Although the photographic chemicals are strong, the method itself is neither difficult nor dangerous. It has been performed in classrooms, homes, and studios without mishap for many years, and it was the day-to-day practice of countless thousands of wood engravers for nearly a century.

It gives engravers the freedom to reproduce anything on wood without having to draw it first. Beginners take delight in having a picture on the block already interpreted into tones and detail by the camera, needing only to be turned into line structures. All of these, and other advantages, make it invaluable.

In practice, few engravers now use the photographic image, but it is nice to know that you can mix up a silver nitrate solution, put rubber bands on a printing frame, and see for yourself the delights of this method.

7 The Basic Technique of Engraving

The first twenty minutes at the workbench can be sheer panic. The engraving tool will not stay in the hand. It feels clumsy and unwieldy, and it may dig too deep into the wood or skid across the surface with no respect for property or flesh. But if you stop and relax for a minute or two, this new endeavor will become much more approachable, and by the end of your first session you will probably have seen at least a glimmer of the glory of engraving.

Naturally, beginners' skills vary. Some will have a dreadful time just making a straight line, while others will casually pick up a tool and delicately cut a flower almost within minutes. Those who have had experience making woodblock prints or linoleum cuts may actually have the most difficulty because the techniques are quite dissimilar and the tools are held and used in a new and different manner.

Proper Position When Engraving

Engraving is most easily done when the whole body is in the right position. Assuming that the light is adequate, the tool sharp and of the proper length, the bench steady, and the block supported at a sufficient height, the proper position for the body is sitting up fairly straight but not rigid in a chair without arm rests. The arms are bent but hanging loosely at your sides, and the elbows are kept free, not resting on the tabletop.

Each line you make in the wood will be *across* the block, from right to left if you are right-handed, and vice versa if you are left-handed. The line is never made up and down on the block.

Holding the Tool

Start with a well-sharpened tool. If possible, have an instructor or more advanced student test its sharpness. There should be no burr on the bottom (you can feel one by rubbing your thumb along the cutting edge at the point). Also, give the tool the fingernail test for sharpness (see page 53). A medium tint tool—No. 3 through No. 6—is ideal, but a split-sticker will also do.

Begin by laying the tool on the table. Grasp it from above with your writing hand, left or right. It will work equally well in either one. Be certain that no fingers are under the cutting edge. After picking up the tool, fit it into your hand with the handle nestled somewhere in the side of your palm just under the little finger, and the point sticking out just beyond your fingers and thumb.

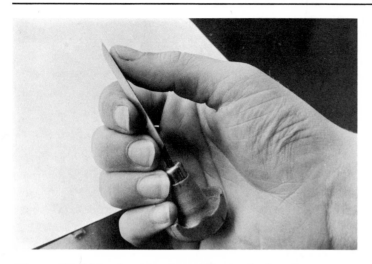

The tool held in the proper position in the hand.

The thumb on one side and the fingers on the other will guide the tool. The palm of your hand will push it forward as you engrave.

Place the tool on a small practice block and attempt to cut a short line. Try not to push with the entire arm as though ironing a shirt. Doing so, of course, will move the tool, but it will not control it. The proper push does not come from the arm or wrist at all, but rather from moving the part of the palm against which the handle rests toward the thumb. This is the essential movement of wood engraving.

At the beginning of the stroke all knuckles are up; at the end of the stroke, the outside knuckle is down, or "in," having pushed the handle toward the thumb.

To visualize the proper hand action, hold the tool first in the air with the fingers on one side and the thumb on the other. Let the thumb stroke up and down on the shank, noting how it moves from in front of your fingers to behind them. Then lay the hand and tool on the block and do the same thing without actually letting the tool cut into the wood, but this time immobilize the thumb with the forefinger of your other hand so that it stays fixed on the block and cannot move. Now, in order to make the thumb stroke the tool, you will have to move the fingers and hand past the thumb.

You see how easy it is?

Once you have this basic motion, cutting a line is easy, and requires almost no effort from the hand or arm.

Position of the Hands on the Block

Old engraving books usually show one hand holding the block and the other hand conducting the tool over its surface. It is possible to cut with only one hand, and in the middle of large blocks, this is the only way, but for proper control, both hands should work together to direct the tool. The illustration shows how the hand holding the block is "connected" to the hand making the engraving by the index finger.

One hand holds the block between the thumb and *second* finger, while the outstretched index finger lies on the block against your other thumb, preventing it from moving. This ensures the proper movement of the cutting hand by keeping the thumb in the same position during the stroke. There is another virtue to this practice—if the tool slips, there is no danger of jabbing the holding hand because it is completely below the surface.

So we have a block held firmly, the tool held firmly, and yet both hands are almost completely at rest.

Making the Line

Wood engravings are made of many single lines, but each line is made of many strokes. Beginners often think that a long line is made by one continuous rapid push, as though the tool were pursuing a fast-crawling insect across the wood. This is not so.

Each stroke is perhaps no more than a quarter of an inch long, but only half of the stroke adds to the length of the line. The other half starts back in the last portion of the line and gives "directions" to the tool hand as the next stroke is made.

This is most easily understood by actually starting a line.

Hold the tool, as described above, ready on the wood, at the top of the block. Lower the point of the tool to the wood at a very slight angle to the surface —almost horizontal—with the handle raised enough to cause the point to catch in the wood. Then push the handle forward gently with the knuckle so that it moves past the thumb in the wood, making a line no longer than a quarter of an inch or so.

Every wood-engraving tool cuts a line of a different depth, and the tool need only enter the wood at a sufficient depth so that you can feel the wood resist slightly as you make your cuts. Having made this first segment of the line, you are ready to make another. Place the point of the tool *back into the segment already cut,* and then push it forward again

The correct position of hands, tool, and block.

another quarter of an inch so that it cuts a little more new line. This is repeated again and again. The tool always goes "one step backward and two steps forward," until the entire line is cut. Thus, what appears to be a continuously engraved line is really a series of "stitches" made in much the same way as with a needle and thread (more about "stitching" later).

Each time you drop the tool back into the line, you can feel it settle into the V-shaped groove already cut. This helps you to keep the same depth throughout the entire line and assists in determining the direction of the next segment.

Chances are your first line was anything but straight. As the tool moved past your thumb in stroke after stroke, each separate one pointed in a slightly different direction. The slightest change in the position of the hand changes the direction of the tool, and therefore of the line. Making a straight line usually takes some practice.

Having completed a single line, the next step is to make another one just like it, and *as close to it as possible*. Start it beneath the first line, and so close that it is just the thickness of a white line away. Try to keep it parallel as you go along. Where the first line zigged, you zig: where it zagged, you zag. Gradually, as you cut line after line, your hand will begin to "understand" what is expected of it, not only for holding the tool, but for guiding it so that the lines become as straight and as parallel and as close together as possible.

All lines on the block are always cut horizontally from the top down. That is, the first line is the highest one, the next line goes under it, and so on. There are no exceptions to this practice. That means that the unengraved wood below the line can be used for the movements of the stitch, and that you move the block around while the tool continues to cut horizontally—from right to left (or left to right if you are left-handed).

Getting the Lines Under Control

Cutting a series of parallel lines is the first exercise for every beginning wood engraver. If the line suddenly goes off the edge of the block, be careful not to jab yourself with the tool.

Beginners almost always make their white lines too far apart. The closer they are to each other, the easier it is to control them, and you can readily see if the new line is getting too close to or far from the previous one. The ideal distance between white lines is a black line so thin that any change in its width is noticed immediately. If your tool starts to break into the black line, stop, redirect it downward, and proceed. Or, if the new white line starts to make a wider black line, you can redirect the tool and straighten the line. Cutting the line in short segments allows you to make these corrections.

It takes a number of engraving hours for all these signals to become automatic in your arm, hand, and fingers. The more you practice making parallel lines,

Print from a single block on which a student has practiced making parallel lines, both straight and curved.

Another student practiced curved parallel lines by making this turtle.

the sooner you will become expert at controlling the tool. This is really the only exercise there is in wood engraving. It is similar to playing the scales on the piano, or hitting the ball against the wall in tennis.

Why should one learn to engrave parallel lines? Why not just make a batch of random lines here and there at will? After all, the student may ask, lines are seldom made parallel in woodblock or linoleum block prints: and besides, doesn't the rigidity of close parallel lines stifle the creative impulse of the engraver?

The answer is threefold. First, the capacity of the wood to hold closely spaced lines gives the wood en-

graver a whole new visual language—the language of *tones*—which produces a quality much more difficult to achieve with woodblock or lino illustrations. Second, even as an exercise, it teaches control of the tool for making *all* lines. Third, the cutting of parallel lines leads to an investigation of a new kind of flat visual space, or of deep visual space. Rather than stifling creative impulses, this exercise opens up new worlds to the creative mind.

In the chapter on tools we talked about the length of the tool and how it affects your control of the line. The best control can be obtained with tools that permit the point to be very close to the thumb.

Any movement of the wrist can cause a tool to change direction ever so slightly, but if the point of the tool is an inch in front of the thumb, this movement of the wrist would cause the tool to move a great deal, giving you very little control.

Learning to "Stitch"

Once you get the hang of making parallel lines, you may want to try to learn to "stitch" as you engrave. This little-used method of cutting lines is very fast, very precise, very rewarding, and makes the cutting of lines almost automatic. Most modern engravers have never heard of it or seen it done, but it was the method once used by all the commercial wood engravers I knew, and was taught to me by my father. Lines made by stitching will be no different in appearance from lines cut in the ordinary way.

Making each segment of the line is like taking a tailor's stitch, which accounts for the name. You make the first segment in the ordinary way. Then, the hand lifts the point of the tool up out of the line only until the point is at surface level. The point is then slid downward and backward and upward in a tiny circle until it rests again in the line, behind the previous end of the line, ready to be pushed forward again for another segment. You hear it click as it drops into the line groove. You push forward. You bring the tool out of the line up the surface, slide it down, back, and up again. Click into the line. And

keep going in this fashion until the line is completed. If you do this on a block that has been inked black, you will see a series of shiny circular marks in the ink down from the line. These are the circles the point has made as it is brought down and back and

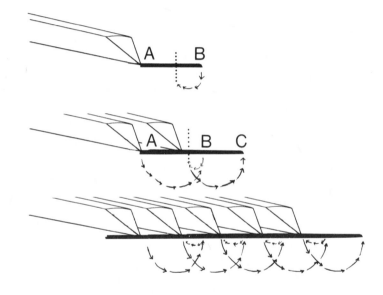

Stitching. The tool is lowered into the wood and pushed from A to B (an actual distance of only ⅛ inch). It is then lifted out and using a circular motion similar to sewing a hem it is returned halfway back toward point A (the dotted line), dropped back into the groove and pushed forward again to C. The process is repeated over and over again until the line is complete.

up again. This stitching method keeps you in control of the line continuously. The little point of the tool never strays far from the line, and the chips that you cut out of the wood seem to drop away from the tool automatically without having to be brushed off or blown away.

Stitching is not everybody's cup of tea, so don't be unhappy if you do not fall into this practice right away. You may find after a while that you are doing it without even thinking about it.

Making a Tint

In music, two notes sounded together are called an interval, and three notes make a chord. The chord made by the three notes is greater to the ear than the notes by themselves because of the relationship of one sound to another.

In wood engraving, two lines close together are the beginning of a relationship, and a third line transforms all three, like a chord, into something greater than the three lines. This relationship is called a tint, because the three (or more) lines fuse into a tone of black that is no longer black or white, but somewhere in between—a gray. It is one of those impossible things that do occur, a mystery performed by the eye that can almost but not quite be explained.

Three lines close together *do* fuse into a tone of gray, darker or lighter, depending on how wide your white lines are and how far apart you have made them. Four lines will make an even better tone, and after that you are off, making a gray tone out of black and white lines as long or wide or dark or light as you wish. It is a very satisfying experience.

When viewed close up, the lines are readily seen, but if you hold the block at arm's length, the lines seem to disappear and a tint is formed. Now look closely at some of the illustrations in this book and discover for yourself that all the "grays" are actually tints made up of many lines.

Needless to say, you will soon tire of making nothing but parallel lines; however, there are all sorts of interesting variations you can try. For example, cut parallel lines in squares, each square going a different way. Also try making each square with a different tool to achieve a different coarseness of tint. By experimenting, you will begin to see the power of your

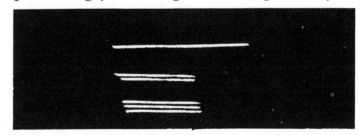

A single line, double line, and triple line made with an angle tint tool. When carefully placed a group of lines will make a gray tone to the eye. This kind of control is easy to obtain by stitching.

tools and understand how they work with one another.

Curved Lines

Sooner or later you will want to make curved parallel lines, and then even concentric circles, and this requires a slightly different technique.

Curved lines are produced by the free movement of the arms, which are not resting on a chair arm or tabletop. The curve is made by starting the tool in a curve, and at the same time, with the other hand, starting the block in an opposite curve against the tool. This produces a twisting movement of the block and tool, which makes the line curve. Pushing the tool in a curve is not enough, and pushing the block in a curve is not enough. Both motions must work into each other.

The curved line is cut, or stitched, in segments, just like the straight line, but as each segment is cut, the elbows are raised a little bit, higher and higher as the movement continues until they are as high as they can comfortably go.

Now, take a large coin or a jar top and draw a circle around it on the wood. Start with a fairly large circle and remember that all your lines are going to be inside it, going from the circumference toward the center. Make your parallel lines as close as you can, and strive for perfect inner circles. *The block must be turned frequently so that you are always cutting at the top of each circle.*

The Ends of the Lines

The beginnings and ends of the lines have their own characters. The end of the line is round where the tool comes out of the wood—because, of course, the point of the tint tool is round. At the beginning of the line there is an "invisible" line where the tool first dropped into the wood, made by that part of the cutting edge that pushes down on the wood just behind the point. This part, called the "bear-down," appears in every line you make, and even though you can't see it easily, it will show up on a proof of the engraving.

Round ends and bear-downs are not real problems for the wood engraver. In many cases they can be totally ignored, especially when using tint tools. The elliptic tools, with their V-shaped cutting edge, however, make bear-downs that more often have to be dealt with.

Most of the lines you make will, of course, be longer than the bear-down. To eliminate the bear-down, make it part of the line. Turn the block around and make one stroke toward the bear-down, removing it entirely. You will have to do this for every line where it shows, but you can wait until an entire passage is completed, and then, turning the block

Tilting the tool to square off the end of a line.

 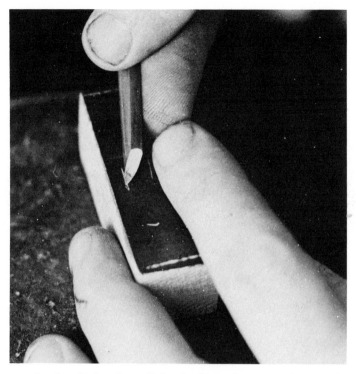

around, do all the bear-downs of that passage at the same time.

There is one other way to get rid of bear-downs, which is usually quite effective. Since the bear-down is actually a dent in the wood, it can be treated in the same way as any dent. Put a drop of water or spit on top of it, let it soak in a little, then wave a lighted match slowly back and forth directly *over* the block, so that the underpart of the flame turns the water to steam, which will swell the pushed-down wood. Do not turn your block upside down to do this. Keep it right side up, in engraving position, using the *bottom* of the match flame.

The round ends of lines are usually quite satisfactory. There are times, however, when you will want a perfectly square line end—for example, when you are cutting letters or small details. To make a square end, tilt the same tool you used to make the line, and jab it gently into all four corners of the line.

In normal wood engraving the tool is always held so that it rides in the wood like a ship in calm water. It does not tilt to either side at all, like a ship leaning from side to side in heavy seas. In making the corners square, however, we must purposely tilt the tool so that its jab into the corners leaves them square—tilting to starboard (right side), so to speak, for the bottom corner, to port (left side) for the upper. (Left-handed engravers will reverse these directions.) As you try this yourself, you will see how easy it is to do. Keep in mind the image of a ship leaning way over, and you will have no difficulty cleaning out the corners of the line.

The Discipline Necessary in Engraving

Something must be said here about the "discipline" of engraving, because the thought may have crossed your mind when you hear words like "perfect" that you are an artistic engraver, not a commercial one, that you want to *enjoy* engraving, not consider it drudgery, and that all your pictures are going to be free and full of life, so you will not need to work on perfect tints or perfect circles or perfect anything else.

We may enjoy driving an automobile, but we enjoy it more the better we know how to operate it. And if you want to play the piano with the abandon of a Beethoven, then you must practice as much as Beethoven did and learn from your predecessors as he did. The "freedom" of Nijinsky's ballet leaps came only with hours of practice every day; and the "freedom" of modern painters came in nearly every case after a long period of academic training.

What appears to be freedom is most often the result of devotion and a lot of hard work. Not unpleasant work, by any means, but serious all the same. No amount of wood-engraving exercises will harm your development as a creative engraver; they can only enhance it. John Farleigh, the British engraver, came to his trade after years of painstaking work as a wax engraver, where forty hours or more of highly detailed work could be melted accidentally and have to be reworked. Stefan Martin, the American wood engraver, whose work is as free in style as his fine paintings, learned wood engraving in a commercial shop, where for four years he apprenticed himself to a rigid, mechanical craft, learning to cut such subjects as lettering microscopes and other scientific instruments for catalogues.

I'm not suggesting that you spend every waking hour practicing parallel lines and concentric circles; but the more you do practice, the better you will engrave and the more you will enjoy it. And in the process of learning, all sorts of new ideas will come to you. Look at the wood engravings of M. C. Escher, and marvel at his precision and exactness. Once you teach the tool to speak, there is no limit to what it can say.

There is a great joy in personal accomplishment, and making simple but perfect parallel lines, or anything else that is painstaking, can be a source of great pride. Practice and experimentation, working something out on a practice block, and making side investigations with the various tools are important and continuous parts of every engraver's learning process. You will increase your manual skill with the tool, as well as your visual-interest involvement. For example, after you make a parallel line tint, you may decide to make another one right over it but at right angles. You will then make the amazing discovery that by doing this you create dots. You might not have known it otherwise. And then, over this double tint, suppose you make yet another tint, this time at a diagonal to the others. What will happen? Will you be amazed again? Will it be like mixing yellow and blue and getting green? Yes, for suddenly a whole new kind of shading dot will appear, this time a diamond or lozenge shape. All sorts of uses for it will occur to you; and you would never have discovered it if you had not been "monkeying around," practicing on your own.

With a little practice, you can duplicate any of the hundreds of tints in the wood engravings shown in this book. You should not try to do them *exactly*, but by looking at them closely, and experimenting on a practice block for a few minutes, you can readily discover how they were done.

8 Advanced Aspects of Technique

Shading

So far, all the tints we have talked about are *flat* tints. They stay the same "color" throughout. Like the individual line made by the tint tool, they do not seem to go toward or away from the viewer, but rather to go across one's plane of vision. There are various tints, however, that go from light to dark. If a single line thickens or thins, it will seem to be coming toward us or going away from us. The wider portion of the line will seem closer, and the thinner portion more distant. If the line swells in the middle and gets thin at the ends, it seems to be coming toward us from a distance and then going away again, and a series of parallel lines has the same effect.

By making lines come toward us and recede again, we are creating a whole new visual idea, the idea of deep space, or a third dimension. Our flat woodblock takes on a potential it didn't have before. It becomes a kind of theater arch or picture window through which we can look into the distance and see some things in front of or behind other things.

Examine the pictures in this book and note which ones seem flat or shallow and which seem deep. Remember that even the deepest picture is cut on a flat two-dimensional surface that has been given the magical property of depth—the third dimension.

What really happens is that we create the illusion of deep space not only by drawing some things in front of others, but also by shading. This movement from dark to light—or light to dark—is movement in and out of our flat plane. Dark lines are thin, and light lines are wide.

In making these lines, instead of using a tint tool, use any of the splitstickers—the elliptic tints. The very nature of a splitsticker helps us move from thin to thick. In fact, with this tool it is difficult *not* to make a line that gets thicker and thinner.

The narrow splitstickers start with a hairline that will get slightly fatter as they cut. A medium splitsticker also starts with a hairline but is capable of making a fatter line. A wide splitsticker still starts with a very fine line and gets very fat. Of course, if we ease any of these tools out of the wood again, the lines will become thin again.

If we use tint tools instead of splitstickers, we can go from light to dark by spacing the lines farther and farther apart. This will create something of the same effect. We can also crossline in two, or even three, directions.

If we use different-width tint tools, even though

we keep the lines the same distance apart, the tint will go from light to dark, which is one reason for keeping a supply of tint tools and splitstickers in a variety of sizes.

Broken Lines and Dots

Tints can also be made by breaking up complete lines. In this way, with a single tint tool (or split-sticker) we can go from dark to light.

We can use dots instead of lines. To make a dot, hold the tool at a greater angle to the wood, as though it were, say, an airplane making a dive. This way only the point digs in and then is lifted right out again.

If we make many dots close together, we produce a very fine dot structure called a *stipple*, which can be flat or can go from light to dark. Multiple lines can go from dark to light too.

The lines and techniques we have discussed represent almost the entire repertoire of strokes and tools. As you become more proficient, you will find ways to enhance these basic ideas and to make shadings of your own.

The Four Basic Forms

Everything that we see every day is in some kind of illumination. Up until a few thousand years ago the sun provided the only source of light, but since then we have added firelight, candlelight, gaslight, and electric light. All of these sources of illumination create lights and shadows on everything we see. The light on an object gives us a clue to its shape, thickness, texture, and movement. Actually, what we see is not the object at all but reflected light. "I do not paint objects," the painter Monet said frequently, "I paint light."

It is the same with the shaded areas that we make on the woodblock. Every stroke makes not only part of the object we are creating but the *light* on that object as well. By depicting the light, we depict the object.

The four basic forms that are components of nearly every object are ball, cylinder, cube, and cone. And if we examine how a single source of light falls on each of these objects, we can learn a great deal about how things are shaded, how they appear to the eye, and how they seem to advance or recede into space as they get lighter or darker.

In a single light source the dark is always on one side, the light always on another. In your own drawings and engravings, be consistent with the shading —the *same side* of everything in the picture must be dark, and the opposite side light. Once again, look through the pictures in this book and see how these dark and light sides produce rhythms of light and dark that add greatly to the drama and the ease of identification. You will also note, especially in the section on student engravings, how when these rules

a. A single line made with an angle tint has the same thickness throughout and appears to be on the same flat plane.

b. A single line made with a splitsticker goes from thick to thin when read from left to right. It appears to recede into space.

c. Also made with a splitsticker, this line swells in the middle appearing to come toward us from a distance and recede again.

d. A group of even, equidistant lines made with an angle tint.

e. A group of lines made with a splitsticker, appearing to go from far to near to far again by going from thin-to-thick-to-thin.

f. A group of curved lines made with a splitsticker.

g. Four lines made with angle tints of different widths, creating the far to near effect.

h. A group of lines of equal width placed farther and farther apart, creating the feeling of a cylinder.

i. A group of lines made with a splitsticker and appearing to come closer by going from thin to thick.

j. By crosshatching, dots are made.

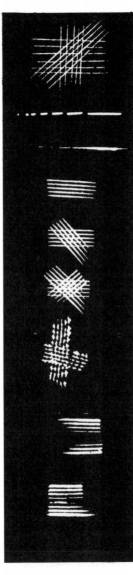

k. Crosshatching at an angle creates diamond shapes and three groups of crosshatched lines break the surface even further.

l. A single line made with an angle tint of even width broken into segments, ending in a dot.

m. A single line made with a splitsticker thinning and ending in wispy segments.

n. A group of lines made with a single stroke of a shooter.

o. One stroke with a shooter cutting diagonally across another making diamond shapes.

p. A third stroke across the first two chews up the diamonds to create an undefined texture.

q. Holding the shooter at a high angle and "walking" or wiggling the tip in the wood creates an unusual dotted group of lines, and "x" crosshatching breaks the surface even further.

r. Leaning the shooter to the top for one stroke creates a group of thick to thin lines and leaning to the bottom creates thin to thick lines.

s. By combining both sets of leaning lines, we come close to cylindrical shading with just two strokes of the shooter.

A picture done entirely in stipple with passages that are almost flat.

are *not* followed the picture is harder for us to "understand" because the shading does not give us the proper light clues.

Negative and Positive Pictures

In almost every visual art we experience, beginning with our very first crayon drawing, the grounds that we work on are white, and the lines that we make are darker than white. In painting, we put **dark paint** on white canvas; in drawing, the dark lines of chalks,

Almost all of the stipple in this portrait was done with the points of a multiple liner tool. The six points of the shooter were diligently and carefully applied to create soft light. Look closely and occasionally you can see the six points lined up.

The first approach to a wood engraving is often a negative picture—a white drawing against a black background.

In this negative picture the interest in shading is apparent. By simply removing the background area, the engraver is on the way to making a positive picture.

pencil, or pen are made on white paper; in etching and in lithography, the lines we make will print as the darks, and what is left remains white.

Not so with wood engraving. Every line we make will print as a white line, and what is left will remain black.

It is easy to think of the block as being a black rectangle, and to leave it black, making white lines in it to represent the drawing. In the beginning most students will make a pencil drawing on an uncoated block, and then engrave the drawing with white lines, each white line appearing where the dark pencil line appeared before. The result is a "negative" picture on the block—a white drawing on a black background. These drawings often have a nice quality of their own, and it can seem as natural to see white lines on black as it does to see black lines on white. Some engravers have great difficulty overcoming this negative idea during their professional lives, while others, from the very beginning, will make only positive engravings. *Right from the start, the student engraver must aim for a picture of black objects on a white ground.* Most of the wood engravings in this book are positive ones. The engraver has treated the subject as though it were on a white background, as in other media.

One good way to think "positive" is to get rid of the black background as soon as possible so that you can visualize what you are doing. Often what looks like a negative engraving is ready to be positive, once the background is removed.

Another way is to understand from the beginning that the lines you engrave are not the lines of the picture but serve to outline the basic drawing. If your drawing is done with lines, then you must cut on each side of the drawn lines so that the drawn lines remain as black.

Texture

One of the great virtues of the wood-engraving

At first glance, this appears to be another negative picture. However, a closer look reveals that the many black areas actually represent dark-shaded areas of the scene depicted, and the intention of the engraver has been to set a dark subject against a light background—a positive picture.

medium is its ability to depict textures with almost unbelievable accuracy. Flesh tones, fur, stainless steel, Scotch plaid, wood grain, tree bark—there seems to be nothing in nature that cannot be cap-

tured on the woodblock with devastating exactness.

Creative engravers seldom make full use of this power, but the masters of the last century and the commercial engravers of today have produced textures that fulfill the potential of the medium. Here are some sample textures taken from sections of commercial blocks done in the last ten years.

It is important for you to see how each texture was accomplished on the block, and to realize that you have both the tools and the skill required to do similar work, although perhaps not as perfectly as the professional.

Actually, it is impossible to make a tint of any kind without the viewer's eye imparting to it some kind of texture. Our eyes want to know what things are made of. And as your tints go from dark to light, their very roughness or smoothness cannot help but suggest the nature of the imaginary surface on which the light is falling.

So after you have learned proper control in the making of parallel lines, spend some spare time making little squares of textures. Scrap blocks will do, or practice on the portions of bigger pictures where the wood is going to be removed later anyway.

Begin by finding a combination of lines, dots, stabs, short strokes, stipple, and so on, which produces the texture you have in mind as though it were a flat surface. Then, try to do it again as though it were going from light to dark. For example, first cut flat bark, then the cylindrical trunk of a tree. Or make something shiny and smooth, and then a shiny, smooth cylinder.

In another exercise, let your tool ply idly in the wood until "accidentally" you discover that what you are making looks like a certain texture. Develop it and explore it more fully. Above all, be certain that you understand what it is about your tones that creates a specific quality. What makes something look "shiny?" What gives the illusion of flesh? How do you depict "gnarled?" How do you give an object the appearance of "transparency?" And so forth. Make a proof of every experiment for your scrapbook.

In this way you will build up a fine vocabulary of wood-engraving techniques, much the same way that a writer builds a vocabulary of words, or a musician one of sounds.

Almost every wood engraving you see will teach you, because each one has something new to say. The visual symbols evoked by line structures are almost unending. In this respect, the classroom or other workshop environment can be most instructive. In a single session you get the benefit of the ideas and experiments of many other engravers. Careful examination of the engravings of masters and professionals is instructive and rewarding.

Textures made with shooters (multiple tools) are often so realistic that the engraver is hard put

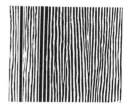

Rough wood. Wood engraving has always had a special affinity for picturing things made of wood. The coarse but carefully made lines create a strong wood grain. The enlarged portion shows how the lines thin out and become broken lines and dots in the shadows.

Smooth wood. The lines here are kept under greater control.

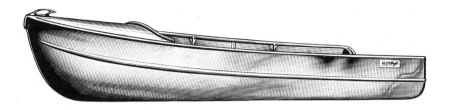

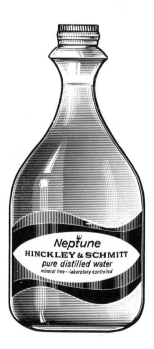

Smooth metal. This aluminum boat makes a dramatic statement. The shading lines have all been cross-lined with a shooter slightly coarser than the horizontal lines.

Glass. The clarity of both the bottle and the water in it is created by using horizontal lines almost exclusively. The bottle highlight was made by cross-lining, but principally by reentering the white horizontal lines and lightening (widening) them.

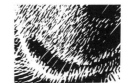

Fur. Short lines simulating the dog's hair are used throughout, except where a stipple retains the different texture of the nose.

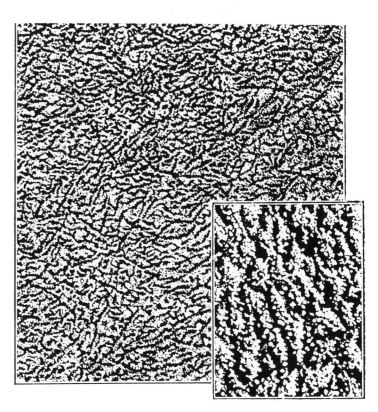

Leather. The texture is a carefully developed pattern of dots, with black areas sharply delineated among the dot clusters. The enlargement clearly shows that the random effect is not really random at all.

Hair and skin. The identical technique was used on both faces, but the lines created by the splitsticker were softened on the woman's face by stippling, and on her hair by cross-lining with a shooter.

Soft cloth. Three techniques have been used to create different qualities and to preserve the texture of the actual material.

to make the other parts of the engraving look as finished. The shooter not only makes lines, crosslines, and diagonal crosslines with great exactness, but its many points can be used to bite into the wood surface and make dots that break up lines into many kinds of softness. Any single tool—shooter, tint, or splitsticker—has a whole new voice when you use it as a stipple, with the point only, breaking up new wood or softening existing lines.

The Magic Square

To take a close-up view of other engravings and to study the technique that was used without becoming distracted by the rest of the engraving, cut a small window—one-half inch by one-half inch—in a piece of paper—eight and a half by eleven inches and place the paper over different parts of engraved pictures. A remarkable thing happens. The picture, which may have seemed quite complex in line structure, will become simple when viewed in a small segment. The overwhelming or awesome techniques of the complete picture are much less formidable when abstracted in a small section. That's why I call the little window a magic square —it unravels the mysteries of the most complicated engraving. Try it out on some of the engravings in this book. I've given you a head start in the accompanying illustrations.

Aspects of Composition

Composition has long been analyzed, and certain rules have been set down. It can be studied at greater length elsewhere, but a brief discussion of it here will help improve your engraving, for when the black and white spaces and lines are working together, an engraving possesses the ability to make a powerful statement.

A pure black square is not very interesting to the eye, but the introduction of almost anything white on the black surface will help it tremendously.

It is the use of white and black in lines and spaces that causes excitement. Some people say they "work together," while others say they "work against each other," but both mean the same thing—the black parts of our engravings enhance the white, and the white enhance the black. And, however subtly they stand side by side, black and white are further enhanced by the addition of a third element—grays, or what we call "middle tones."

These middle tones are the "tints" discussed earlier. The eye of the viewer blends the black and white lines to produce light and dark grays that help to soften the larger areas of black and white, although sometimes we want the shock of pure black against white.

The picture of the checkers player was made by a student during his fourth or fifth sessions. Being a

Checker player made by one of my students.

the composition. The black and white areas are just about equal, but there are so many different shapes, textures, and ideas that the composition does not hold together with any power at all. Squares, diagonals, nongeometric shapes, deep space at the front, shallow space at the rear, and the black wall dominating the picture confront the eye. This is actually *two* pictures, the top half being quite complete without the bottom half. The figure of the man would be very good even without the background. Despite my criticism, both the student and I were delighted with the engraving. It showed promise, and he has since gone on to make very exciting engravings.

Incidentally, the darkening of the edges of the man's sleeves was done with a burnisher, to give some three-dimensional form to the figure.

Learn by observing the technique and composition in the successful and powerful engravings of the masters, past and present. Many are represented in this book.

beginner, he was interested in using his new tools to make a picture but not overly concerned yet about

9 Proofing in Black and White

After the image has been drawn on the block and cut, the next and often final stage is proofing—inking and printing the block—making proofs, or "pulls," as the English say. Some engravers wait until the block has been completely cut before proofing it, while others like to make proofs along the way to check their progress or alter the image.

Inking

The work space should be prepared by positioning the inking slab, block, and press or proofing jig within easy reach of each other, as described in Chapter 5. Blocks can be inked without being removed from the press or jig, but many engravers prefer to place the block adjacent to the inking slab (which is slightly below the height of the block) so that the brayer will roll over both slab and block at the same time. Most wood engravings are not much larger than four by six inches and it is easy to ink them at the slab with six to twelve strokes of the brayer.

With a pallette knife or some kind of small spatula, remove a tiny bit of ink from the can and place it on the brayer, not directly on the slab. Then roll the brayer back and forth across the slab until the ink is spread into a thin, even film. Raising the brayer at the end of each stroke to let it spin before taking another stroke helps to spread the ink faster.

Too much ink will put too much ink on the block and will fill in some of the lines of your image, while too little ink will result in proofs that are not as rich as they should be. It's better to start with too little ink, however; you can always add more if you need it, but once you've overinked, you'll have to clean the surfaces of both the block and the slab. The proper amount will make a slight hissing sound as the brayer rolls back and forth. Also remember that you only need to cover an area on the slab the width of the roller, and about two inches wider than the block. We've already discussed the kind of stiff printer's ink used in engraving and I'll only repeat here that the soft inks used for wood-block and linoleum-block printing will not work at all in the delicate lines of a wood engraving.

If you have over-inked the block, or you've finished making all the proofs you want, the best way to remove the ink is to proof it off. Run the block through the press a few times with newsprint paper

Inking the roller.

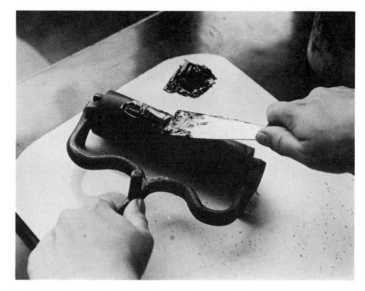

Spreading the ink on the slab.

over it until most of the ink is removed and only a faint image prints. The remaining ink can be removed with a soft rubber eraser, such as Pink Pearl brand. A typewriter eraser will not do because of its scratchy quality. Using an eraser eliminates the need for solvent of any kind. Solvent it not only harmful to inhale and irritating to the skin and eyes, but when used on the wood-engraving block it washes ink down into the lines and detracts from the visual excitement of the block by eliminating the light lines in the otherwise dark block. Solvent will not actually

harm the wood, and it can be used to remove ink that has not dried, but it's just not the best way.

Proofing Without a Press

If your block is no larger than four by five inches it is very easy to lay paper directly upon the inked block and rub the back of the paper with a kitchen spoon. If you put several sheets of newsprint or other soft paper over the block, you can get a fair proof by using a kitchen rolling pin. Place strips of wood, the same height or slightly lower than the block, ad-

Inking the block.

"Locking up" the block with magnets. Pieces of furniture separate it from the sides of the jig.

jacent to the top and bottom edges of the block so that when the rolling pin reaches the end of the block it will drop only slightly if at all and will not tear the proofing paper.

A more sophisticated method of proofing for engravers who haven't a platen or cylinder press is with a device called a proofing jig. It can be handmade (see page 65) or bought ready-made (see Appendix). With the jig, the block is inked, placed in position on the bed, and held there by strong magnets. It is covered with a piece of proofing paper that is held in place by spring clips, so when you lift the paper to see how the proof looks, it will always fall back on the block in exactly the same place. A kitchen spoon or a burnisher is used to rub evenly over the entire surface of the paper covering the block. Proofing is made even easier and faster by putting a sheet of acetate over the paper and placing a drop or two of oil on the acetate to remove all friction as you rub.

While it is easy to imagine a big iron press smashing down the lines of an engraving, even a burnisher

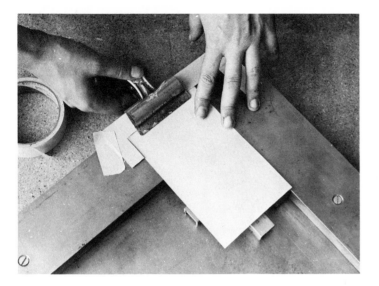

One way of positioning the paper over the block. The L-shaped piece of mat-board allows you to place the paper in register each time you proof.

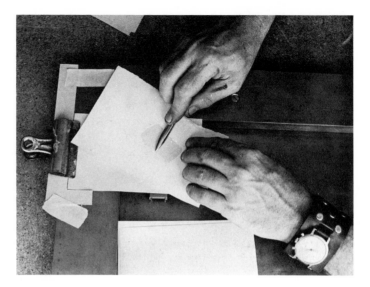

Proofing. Rub a burnisher or the bowl of a spoon over the block. A second sheet of paper will protect your proofing paper.

or spoon can be pushed too hard on the surface of the block and flatten the highest part of the lines so that they become wider, and therefore print darker, and the spaces between them become narrower. Unless you want this darkening effect (and often engravers deliberately press too hard in order to make certain passages darker), be careful when proofing with a burnisher, especially in the delicate areas of the block. After all, the block is just wood, and while its end-grain characteristics make it sturdier than plank-

grain wood, it can still be damaged.

Proofing with a Press

Wood engravers may find access to a good working press through a high school or college print shop. Instructors are often anxious to incorporate the printing of wood engravings into their activities and may be willing—perhaps even eager—to allow an aspiring wood engraver to use the press. It's an avenue worth investigating. Private print workshops usually

Another method of positioning the block and paper. A piece of furniture is taped to the iron bed, and register pins are taped to it. Holes punched in your proofing paper will fit over the register pins and position each sheet in exactly the same place for every proof you pull.

Here the register pins have been taped to the side of the jig.

have cylinder proof presses too, and some of the grander ones may even have a Washington (platen-type) proof press available, although so long as a press operates properly, no one press is any better than another.

Most of the proofing of wood engravings is done on cylinder presses simply because they are the easiest to find and the least expensive. Commercially, they are used to proof cuts and type, or just type in galleys so that the printer can see what sort of words or images the material being proofed contains. In some of the older cylinder presses the heavy cast-iron roller is not attached in any way to the bed of the press, and if a block or piece of type is too high, the roller merely rises a little to accommodate it. The cylinders of presses of any value to the wood engraver roll in a fixed track over the block and will not move upward even slightly to accommodate anything. The gap between the cylinder and the bottom of the bed of the press is always a bit wider than the height of type (.918 inch) so that

Pulling a proof on a cylinder press.

Proofing with a frisket over the block.

several sheets of paper can be placed over the block; and since the presses were made to proof type, they are usually high enough to accommodate the proofing stick as well, which enables the printer to make corrections while the type is in the press.

The simplest proofing press has a small cylinder encased in a rubber padding, the diameter ranging from an inch to four inches. These presses are often used by department stores to print display signs but they are also ideal for proofing wood engravings. Larger cylinder proof presses have devices for wrapping paper (called packing) around the cylinder, while others have grippers for positioning and securing the proofing paper, or devices for proofing in register. The operation of these presses will vary slightly from model to model but it is usually a simple procedure with rules that can be determined readily. I would need the space of another book to discuss the different presses and give instructions for their use, and here I prefer to concentrate on those things that every wood engraver needs to know.

Applying Pressure

You can damage the lines of your engraving when

proofing by hand but you run an even greater risk when proofing in a large press. In a platen press excessive pressure comes from squeezing too hard when you pull the lever that lowers the platen onto the block. Always start with light pressure until you find the right amount for the block you are proofing. Pressure is not determined by the size of the block but by the amount of solid black area left on the surface. Large areas of solid black will require much more pressure than delicate traceries of lines.

With cylinder presses it is important to build up the packing papers under and over the block gradually, so that the block is never squeezed too tightly between the immovable press bed and the unyielding cylinder. The result can easily be smashed lines on your engraving.

Makeready

Even though modern processes are often used in the manufacture of wood engraver's maple and boxwood, every engraver will soon discover—when making the first proof with a new block—that the blocks are not always of uniform height. Certain areas—one corner, for example—may be thicker or thinner than the rest of the block and when proofed in a press will appear darker or lighter than other sections. The height may actually vary as much as .030 inch from corner to corner.

When proofing by hand, this won't interfere with the clarity of your proofs, but when proofing in a

press, some kind of compensation must be made to level the surface by raising the lowered parts. Often simply placing a thin piece of paper, called makeready paper, under the low spot will do the trick. Thin tissue paper, newsprint paper, the pages from an old telephone directory, or Kleenex are all suitable as makeready paper. If you find that more than one piece of paper is needed, start with a small one and gradually add pieces that are slightly larger than the last so that the pressure of the press on the wood will be spread out and even. A small stack of paper the same size under the block would have the same effect as accidentally placing the block on a coin, matchstick, or something similar in the press. The pressure of the cylinder could easily crack the block.

In some cases a high portion of the block can be lowered by rubbing the underside of the high spot with a piece of coarse sandpaper. In this way an entire block can be lowered several thousands of an inch in less than a minute.

Masking

There are times when the engraver would like to proof only part of the block, perhaps because only part of the drawing has been engraved, or to see what the central portion looks like without a background. Whatever the reason, this is accomplished by masking.

One method is to mask out part of the image so

that only the desired area will print. Before you ink the block, cover the unwanted portion of the surface with paper. The brayer will roll over both block and masked area but only the unmasked area of the block itself will be inked. Remove the mask and make your proof. This method is fine if you want only one proof; it becomes unwieldy for more than one because you will have to make a new mask for every proof you pull.

Another way to mask is to make a frisket. Ink and proof the block on newsprint paper and then carefully cut out of the proof the part of the image that you want to isolate and print separately. The remaining part of the newsprint proof is the mask, or frisket. After you ink the block, place the frisket on the wet ink and the proofing paper over the frisket. Now when you proof, only the part of the image that appears through the hole in the frisket will actually print. A frisket can be used over and over again.

Proofing Large Blocks

Some engravers work with blocks as large as twelve by twenty-four inches. The size makes them difficult to proof on either platen or cylinder presses, not only because of warpage, but because so few of the simpler presses have beds large enough to handle these blocks. One engraver solved the problem by using a stone lithographer's press, dampening the paper, and letting the scraper blade of the press make a proof just as it does from the lithographer's

stones. Most engravers usually hand-rub all their large proofs, even for editions of one hundred copies. While time consuming, this is a safe and effective way to proof large blocks.

Proofing Warped Blocks

Both the upper and lower surfaces of the blocks constantly absorb and evaporate moisture for the life of the block. If one surface absorbs or evaporates more moisture than the other, the block will curl slightly or warp, making it difficult or even impossible to proof. As noted in an earlier chapter, warpage can be avoided by properly storing the blocks in a vertical position so that both surfaces are always exposed to the same atmosphere.

You can always hand-rub a warped block in a proofing jig if you need a proof before you have time to remove the warp. Also, if the block is warped from side to side so that its curve matches the curve of the cylinder on a press you can carefully proof the block on the press, making certain that the cylinder follows the warpage. If the curl is downward, you can proof the block upside down on proofing paper placed in the bed of the press.

If all four corners of the block are warped inward so that the curve is like that of a ball, the block cannot be proofed on any kind of press until the warp has been removed. To flatten such a block, or any kind of warped block, place it above a dish of water with the inward part of the curve toward the dish. Within a few hours the grain will have absorbed enough water to straighten out—if left a few more hours it may even curve the other way! So keep a close watch as you remove the warp.

Multiple Proofing

Almost all proofs are made singly, one to each sheet of paper, but many unusual and interesting effects can be obtained by proofing the same block several times on the same sheet of paper, or even by proofing different blocks on the same paper. By reinking the block and repositioning the paper over it so that the images are adjacent, overlapping, or whatever, unpredictable and often exciting proofs are made. A whole art form can be created out of multiple proofing a single block, or combining it with lead type or other kinds of type-high printing plates.

Proofing an Edition

An almost unlimited number of impressions can be made from a wood engraving without the slightest visible difference between the first impression and the last. In 1973 an edition of proofs from the blocks of Thomas Bewick were published by the Newberry Library of Chicago after being painstakingly made ready and proofed by R. Hunter Middleton. The edition was lauded worldwide as even better than those taken by Bewick himself, nearly a hundred and fifty years before.

Sooner or later every engraver will want to pull an edition from one of his own blocks and label it as such. An authentic edition may either be hand-inked and rubbed by the engraver himself or mechanically inked and proofed in a press by a professional printer, so long as the engraver has supervised the printing and the proofs are made directly from the block. It is no discredit to have a professional do all the engraver's printing. In fact this was once the general practice, and today, at Tamarind Lithography Workshop on the West Coast and at University Limited Art Editions in the East, master printers pull all the impressions from the stone, under the watchful eye of the artist who signs and numbers the finished prints. Editions can number five prints, or one hundred, or several thousand. The fewer there are, of course, the more valuable they become.

The rules for making editions have been established by printmaking societies:

1. Each print must show the number of that individual print, the total number of prints in the edition, and be signed by the artist. The usual style is: *3/30 David M. Sander*, indicating that the print is the third one in an edition of thirty made by David M. Sander.

2. After the edition is printed, the block should be marred or altered in some way so that no further proofs can be made. A great X through the center of the block will do the trick. This is to guarantee the authenticity of the edition for future purchasers of the prints.

3. A very small number of "artist's proofs" can be made, for the artist to give to friends, without diminishing the value of the edition. They should be labeled as such.

An edition must be made in a single session at the press. From a purist point of view, coming back the next morning is the same as coming back ten years later. During the passage of time, however short, something may have changed—the paper, the ink, or the amount of pressure you give the proofs—which makes the later proofs different from the earlier group. Purists argue that everyone who owns one of your numbered proofs is entitled to believe that it is identical with every other print in the edition. No changes may be made after you start. Therefore, eliminate any proofs that are different—either by destroying them or by calling them "artist's proofs."

You can make later editions from a block but they must be labeled to indicate that they are not the first edition; for example: *Second Edition/3/20 David M. Sander*. You can also make special editions and name them accordingly—*Birthday Edition, School Edition*, or whatever.

Once you have made an edition, you have also made a commitment to your work and to those who own the prints. If it were otherwise, assuming your work is in demand, you might be able to crank out a few more prints any time you need more income, almost as though you had your own money-printing

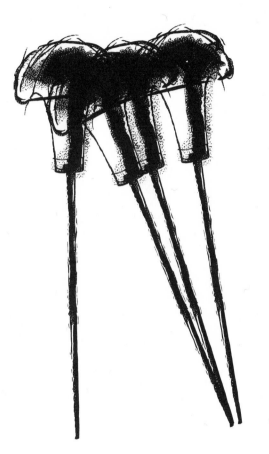

An example of multiple proofing.

press. Obviously this would be cheating those who believed they were buying part of a truly limited edition.

10 Proofing in Color

Colored Papers and Inks

Great visual excitement can sometimes be created by proofing in color. The simplest way is to proof on papers of different colors, using black ink. You will create different effects when you proof on light paper stocks like cream, buff, gray, and tan. The colored stock will decrease contrast because it eliminates pure white, but it adds its unique qualities, which may suit your style or purpose even better.

Another simple experiment with color is using colored inks and proofing in as light and dark hues as are available. Any printer's ink used for offset or letterpress printing will do, and since a dab of any color is all you need, perhaps you can get some cast-off cans from small commercial printers instead of buying full ones.

Printer's ink has the same qualities as the proofing ink you have been using, with one important difference—it dries rapidly. It will stay wet for only an hour or two and must not be left on the slab or roller overnight. If it does dry, you will have to use a strong solvent to remove it. Remember to wear rubber gloves when using solvents and to keep the window open because solvents are harmful to inhale and can irritate the skin. It's obviously far better to clean everything as soon as you have completed a proofing session and to use a relatively weak solvent to do so. Clean the block carefully after each color to avoid a buildup of dried ink which, when it gets thick enough, will become a new printing surface that no longer actually represents your lines.

It is also a good idea to start with light colors and add darker ones later. That way you can change the color on the slab by adding another without cleaning everything in the process. Inks can be mixed on the slab by placing a dab of one color on a dab of another right on a corner of the slab and thoroughly mixing the two with your pallette knife until you get the color you want. To test it, "tap out" the color by touching the ink lightly with the tip of your forefinger and tapping your finger on a piece of proofing paper until the ink is spread out as thin as it will be when rolled on the slab. In this way you can quickly tell if the color is right, and avoid the frustration of rolling the ink out only to find that in a thin film the color is different from the thick puddle you started with.

By combining colored inks and colored paperstocks you can pursue a range of ideas and will find that the possibilities become almost limitless. You can also increase your color vocabulary by altering the pure black ink, adding colors to it, and proofing in these new varieties of off-black. For example. a touch of brown mixed with black makes a brownish-black that prints beautifully on white or tan paper. Black mixed with yellow will give you a kind of dark green. Mixed with other colors, the variations are endless. You will always retain the strength of the black while adding the charged feeling of color. Next, experiment with mixing white into your black ink to obtain various shades of gray.

Proofing in Register

In all color work where more than one color is used, the proofing must be done in register; that is, the block must print on the same place on every sheet of paper. Although this may seem almost impossibly complicated, it is actually quite simple, requiring one of several mechanical devices for positioning the block and the paper in exactly the same place in the press or proofing jig.

In a cylinder press the block is held securely in the same spot on the iron bed by pieces of furniture pressed tightly against it on all four sides with powerful magnets. It cannot move in any direction except up, allowing us to remove it for inking at the slab and to drop it back in place again.

Putting the paper down in the same place is somewhat more complicated. Some presses have grippers that can be adapted for this purpose, but a piece of wood furniture taped to the bed of the press with register pins taped to it will serve your purpose just as well. The proofing paper, which is punched, either by hand or in a two-hole punch, will then drop onto the register pins perfectly again and again. After all the colors are proofed, the register holes are cut off the print.

In a proofing jig the situation is quite similar. The block is locked on the bed with magnets and register pins are taped to the lip. Another method is to cut an "L" out of mat board and tape this to the lip, positioning the corner of your proofing paper in the inside corner of the "L" and securing the paper by clamping it to the lip with spring clips.

If whatever device you are using does not slip, the image you are proofing will appear in the same place on the paper again and again. Another way to ensure that your work is in register is by making register marks in the block itself (this will be discussed a little further along).

Proofing over a Tone Block

One way to enhance the pure black of an engraving is to proof it over a solid tone of some very light color. Traditionally, a light yellow, buff, or tan is used, but any color will do as long as it's light. The tone block needn't be end-grain wood because it will not be cut but will be printed as a solid color.

This hamburger was printed in two colors. First, the entire image was engraved on one block—the key plate. This image was then transferred to a second block—the color plate—which was engraved to give highlights and add color to the bun and filling. The color plate was then proofed several times and the key plate proofed in black over the color.

It is usually a tiny bit larger—one-sixteenth of an inch or so—than the engraved block, which is called the "key plate" in color work. The tone block is printed first on a number of sheets of proofing paper that are allowed to dry for several hours, even overnight. Some colors dry faster than others and you might test them if you are in a hurry.

The tone block is removed from the press and cleaned, and the key plate is then laid down. Position the solid tone over the key plate so that it is as perfectly centered as possible. This will take some practice, which is one reason for proofing many more sheets of the tone block than you are likely to want. This simple experiment will show how a faint sug-

gestion of color will "set off" the black in an exciting way. There are several reasons for this. The film of black ink has been separated from the paper surface by the faint tone underneath, and the tone around the outside of the black plate acts as a frame or border. While the tone itself is invisible in the black areas, it is clearly visible in the highlights, which now appear in color instead of pure white.

A darker tone under the black will produce a different effect. Use the tone block to experiment with proofing color under the key plate until you know all the different "voices" that this kind of simple color proofing can provide. Of course, the key plate does not have to be black. In fact, a dark-colored key plate

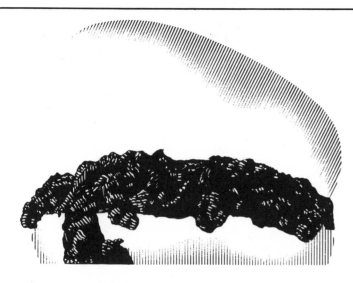

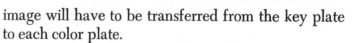

printed over a light solid tone of the same color is often very dramatic and quite interesting. Remember, though, that the darker the tone block, the darker the highlights will be, and some of the vitality of the original engraving may be lost. The next two methods of color proofing—with several plates and by reduction—allow you to work with a dark tone and still keep the highlights pure white.

Color Proofing with Several Plates

With this method you will need a separate same-size block for each color. Since part of the image—often overlapping parts containing highlights or shading—will be engraved on each of the blocks, the complete

image will have to be transferred from the key plate to each color plate.

The key plate is first engraved completely, and register marks are cut into the margin in the center of at least two sides of the plate. The traditional register mark is a circle with a cross in it. The key plate is then inked with black ink and proofed on a piece of clear acetate, which is held firmly by hand to keep it from moving and proofed by rubbing with a spoon or burnisher. Now the acetate with the wet image on its underside is lifted off the key plate and carefully laid down on a blank block. Again, it is rubbed with the burnisher and this time the image and register marks are transferred from the acetate

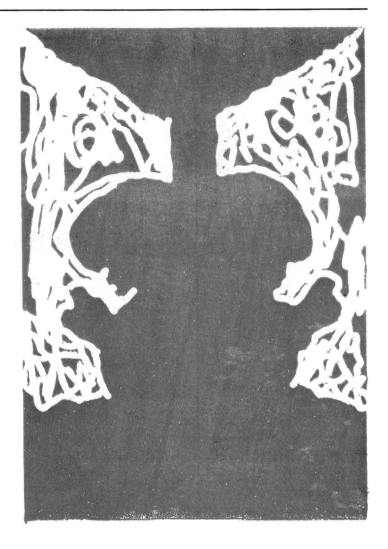

This engraving was made by reduction. The image was drawn on the block and the background engraved (in this case with a router), and several proofs were made. The background area was then completely removed from the block and the two figures and tree were engraved. These were proofed in register over the background proofs to give two colors plus white. By proofing a tone block before engraving and proofing the background, you would produce three colors, but you would lose the white.

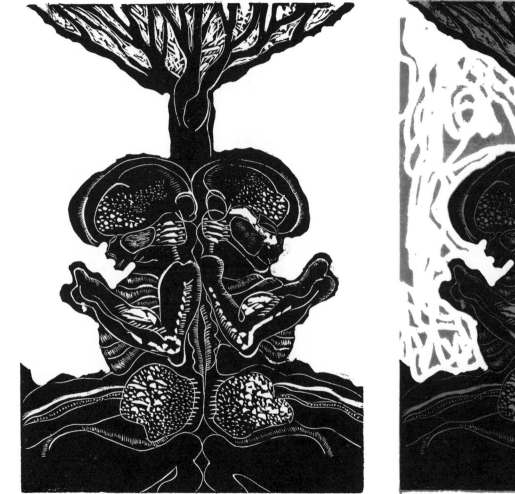

to the new block, which will be the color plate. With the exact image on the color plate, it can be engraved to print color just in those areas where you want color, highlights, or shading. Be certain to cut the register marks on this block.

The color plate is proofed before the key plate. Be sure to make more proofs than you think you'll need to allow for spoilage. After you've finished proofing, punch another sheet of acetate, place it on the register pins, and proof it exactly like a regular proof. Now remove the color plate and drop in the key plate, placing the acetate proof sheet over it. You can now move the key plate around slightly to position it so that its register marks line up exactly with the register marks on the acetate impression of the color plate. If you lock it in that exact position, your first proof and every subsequent one will be in perfect register. Usually, however, it takes a little adjustment left and right, or up and down, before the position is perfect. This is what causes the spoilage and why you should make many proofs of the color plate. The only sure way to tell whether the key plate is in the right position is to pull a proof or two, but this punched acetate method helps to cut down on the spoilage.

Color Proofing by Reduction

In the reduction block process the same block is used to cut and proof the colors. Part of the image is cut and proofed. It is then removed completely from the block and another part of the image is cut and proofed over the previous color. This technique has its virtues but also one obvious drawback. Once the first image has been proofed and either removed or altered to make the second image, the first image can never again be proofed. It has been destroyed forever. The main virtue is that a carefully planned set of proofs can be executed quite quickly in two, three, or even more colors. Register problems are almost eliminated because the block is simply dropped back into exactly the same place for every proof. No transferring of the image from one block to another is needed. And finally, in working directly over the same image, you can develop a strong sense of continuity and feel in closer touch with your work.

Perhaps the technique is most clearly understood by studying the illustrated example here. The first color was actually a solid orange, made by proofing the entire block as a tone block. Twenty-five proofs were made. Then part of the block was removed for the second color, the background. In this case the actual work was done in five minutes with a printer's routing machine. Seventeen of the original twenty-five survived proofing with the second color. Then the entire background area was removed with the router, and the main image—the two figures and tree

—was engraved and printed in black. In this example only three good prints survived the entire process. Even so, since it was the first attempt by one of my students at color proofing using this method, it was remarkably successful.

Frisket Proofing

One last and simple color-proofing technique is called "stopping out" or frisket proofing, which requires only one block. Make a frisket exactly as you did when masking sections of the block in black-and-white proofing (see page 119). This time cut around the part of the proofed image that you want to print in color and keep both parts of the mask you cut out. First proof the color area through the window, making several proofs. Then, after cleaning the block and inking it with your second color (or black) place the piece that you cut out on the wet ink over the area it fits and proof the second color over the first. Or, you can make a second frisket masking out the area you printed in the first color.

To print this scene in two colors, the engraver first masked the Indians with a frisket and proofed the background in brown. Next, the background was masked and the Indians were proofed in black over the brown proofs.

11 A Portfolio of Style

The Water Tower *by Asa Cheffetz. This extraordinarily fine and sensitive engraving is by another regional artist, who told the story of New England, of the rural countryside and the weatherbeaten structures reflecting man's struggle with an often harsh environment.*

Bookplate by Boyd Hanna.

Bookplate for Hudson's Bay Company by John DePol.

These two bookplates show different approaches to a practical piece of work—one highly detailed and the other quite simple. Bookplate societies and clubs are found in many countries of the world, and in some of them more than a dozen artists cut work in wood and metal. Bookplate engraving can be a lucrative source of income for enterprising wood engravers, and the finished proofs are often sold and traded like coins or stamps.

After Landscape with Polycrates Receiving the Fish *by Salvator Rosa. (Courtesy of The Art Institute of Chicago.) My father, Jacob Sander, whose work appears elsewhere in this book, apprenticed himself to the wood-engraving trade in 1895. He always preferred portraits and landscapes to mechanical subjects, and his firm, founded in 1919, not only did "artistic" subjects for its own clients but often for other wood-engraving firms as well. When he wasn't working on a customer's block, he had photographs put on wood so that he could work on them in the evenings at home. This engraving from Rosa's painting was made in 1951, the last year of his life. The unimportant details are minimized, while maximum attention is given to the action in the painting and a strong dimensional quality is created by the use of dark against light, and dot against line.*

Fields *by Garrick Palmer.*

House *by Rosemary Kilbourn. This artist creates bold engravings with vigorous lines and much movement.*

Here, the clouds, trees, and land seem more muscular than and fully as substantial as the wooden building.

Note how variations on the same basic technique are used to differentiate the hair, flesh, soft cloth background, and nubby sweater. (*Engraved by Jonas Tricis.*)

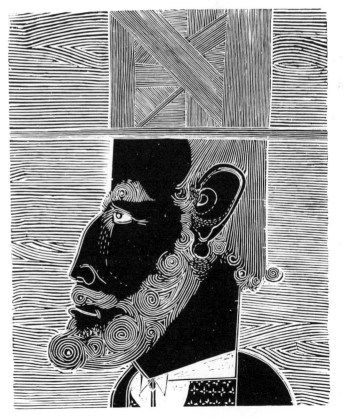

An apprentice in the shop relieved the boredom of practicing cutting parallel and curved parallel lines by working on this design. The entire surface seems flat, with everything on exactly the same plane. This effect is created by tints that do not become darker or lighter. (Engraved by Robert Billings.)

A *portrait of Floyd Patterson, the prizefighter, in which the sparkle of light determined the technique. It solves the difficult problem of how to turn a face into line structures without the lines appearing to be the actual, natural lines on a real face. The technique results in a strong and dramatic portrait. (Engraved by Glen Jeskey.)*

Three portraits by Leonard Baskin. His many wood engravings are far less known than his drawings, lithographs, and sculptures. In these calligraphic and personal images Baskin employs the technique of wood engraving to reproduce his unusual drawing style.

The best of the "old" style of the commercial wood engraver working in the 1920s is shown in this bathing beauty. The entire picture was made with a variety of splitstickers and every area is toned in the manner of a photograph, with no pure black or white areas. Note the strong sensuousness of the left arm, and the delicate cross-lining of the shoulder and legs.

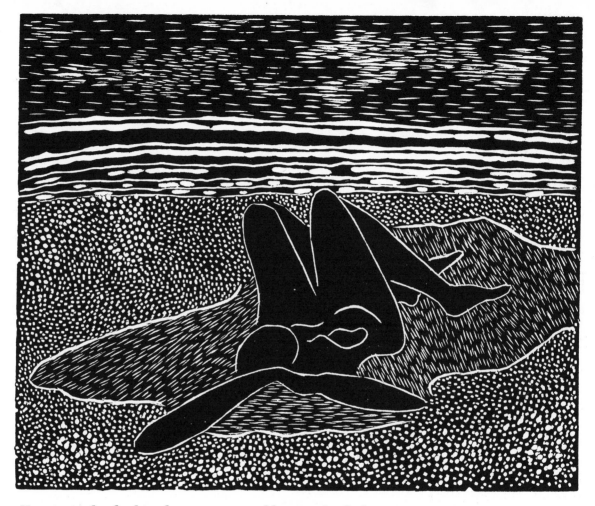

Here is another bathing beauty, engraved by one of today's creative engravers, Inara Cedrins. Her approach is quite different and reveals the flexibility of the medium.

One virtue of wood engraving is that the texture of the
wood surface does not show in the finished proofs, but
here the engraver has deliberately scraped areas of the
wood with a wide, flat graver to create a new texture.
You can see this in the area just below the left ear, on
the middle back, front haunch, and lower left leg of the
boldly wrought rhinoceros.

The wood-engraving medium also lends itself to more nostalgic subjects and styles. These engravings from the 1950s have captured the look of old-time work. (Sun by R. Goltz. Ship by N. Paul Quirk. Paper maker by Glen Jesky.)

These three engravings are from France, where wood engraving is often used to interpret watercolors, pencil sketches, and ink drawings with great sensitivity. These are so close in feeling to the other media that it's hard to believe they are actually wood engravings.

APTEMIƧ

J.R. '49

The New South Wales Wolf *engraved two centuries ago by Bewick to illustrate his* Quadrupeds (1790).

Artemis *by Imre Reiner. Mr. Reiner, a typeface designer turned wood engraver, uses the multiple liner "as though it were a brush," says one reviewer, who failed to note that Reiner has used only the single tool in this and other work.*

Detail of Rooster *by Stefan Martin. This is a fine example of Martin's use of solid and broken lines.*

Fred Brian, an Illinois engraver, made this dramatic picture for a portfolio he put together, writing the text, setting the type, and printing it by hand.

Frog *by Stefan Martin. The technique here is quite different from that used in his* Rooster.

Passion Flower *by Leon Gilmour. The flower itself may be highly detailed, but the engraver has made a strong statement of solid black and white.*

Wood engraving has its lighter side.
(Engraved by Elgas Grim.)

J. J. Lankes, a great regional artist, took up wood en-
graving in the 1920s and illustrated many books, notably
the poetry of Robert Frost. Most of his work is taken
from nature, but this one has such a holiday spirit that
it seems appropriate to include it here as an example
of the kind of Christmas card engravers can create.

Betty Prior Rose *by G. Brender à Brandis. A variety of tools and techniques were used to make this picture exciting. Even the spaces between leaves and flowers vibrate with an engraver's energy.*

Appendix: On Becoming an Engraver

Twenty-five years ago I heard a professor of English tell a poetry class that only two poets in America—Robert Frost and Ogden Nash—made a living by their poetry. Only two, and yet no one was discouraged. Most of the students didn't write poetry to sell anyway, but for the sheer expressive joy of it.

There may be as few as two people making a living by their wood engraving—perhaps less than two dozen in the entire world. And yet thousands of wood engravers are at work, enjoying their self-imposed task, and delighting in giving or trading proofs or prints, or in making an occasional sale to a museum or through a gallery. Some of the lucky ones may illustrate pamphlets and books, but the pay is lean and there is seldom a backlog of orders.

Many wood engravers teach wood engraving one or two days a week, some at university print departments, others at neighborhood workshops or in their own homes. Most engravers, however, work for the rewards of the work itself. Even so, there are a few traditional outlets that you may consider.

Bookplates, for example, can be designed and engraved in just a few hours. One famous artist/engraver is paid several hundred dollars for the block and one hundred plates, signed in the block itself.

Greeting cards are another potential source of income. You can begin by making your own and in time perhaps build up a clientele. You might then be able to interest a local museum store or card shop in carrying your work.

Local advertising agencies, publishers, and even printers may be interested in knowing about a source for wood-engraving illustrations. We have not mentioned that wood engravings are sometimes used in offset printing (often called "lithography"), where they are photographed and printed from the photographic impression. Using photography, the wood-engraving image can be enlarged, reduced, repeated, rendered in color, or in variations of black and color tones. Whatever the original size and color may have been, it can become a broadside, poster, or even billboard. Commercial artists find that making a picture on a woodblock often renders the picture much more interesting—an advantage in the competitive illustration market. Some wood engravers even take their equipment—press and all—to art fairs in the summertime and engrave in the open air, while patrons view the framed prints displayed around them.

I'm not encouraging you to follow a commerical path, but it is possible for the ambitious. The medium is flexible enough to suit your personal needs, whatever they may be.

Sources for Supplies

Retail

American Printing Equipment Company, 45–25 9th Street, Long Island City, New York 11101. (212) 982-2265. *Manufactures maple blocks needing considerable sanding before use.*

Brookstone Company, Inc., 127 Vose Farm Road, Peterborough, New Hampshire 03458. *Sells the sharpening jig (referred to as Plane and Chisel Honer in catalogue), which can be adapted to wood engraving tools. Catalogue available.*

Andrews/Nelson/Whitehead, 31–10 48th Avenue, Long Island City, New York 11101. (212) 937-7100. *This fabulous paper company imports a vast array of tissue and other special papers from many countries. Write for samples.*

Graphic Chemical and Ink Company, P.O. Box 27, 728 North Yale, Villa Park, Illinois 60181. (312) 832-6004. *Although principally a supplier of materials for etching and lithography, this firm sells maple and boxwood blocks and long engraving tools that will require shortening. Write for catalogue.*

J. Johnson & Company, 132 Adams Avenue, Hempstead, New York 11550. (516) 292-1843. *Johnson has been making boxwood blocks since the early 1900s. Also sells maple blocks and Muller tools (which will need shortening) and other accessories.*

The Sander Wood Engraving Company, 212 Lincoln Street, Porter, Indiana 46304. (219) 926-4929. *I established this company in 1972 to meet the needs of wood engravers, to supply tools of the right length and shape, woods, inks, sharpening jigs, proofing jigs, and other necessities. Virtually all the materials described in this book are in stock. Write for catalogue.*

Wholesale

Edward C. Lyons, 16 West 22 Street, New York, New York 10003. (212) 982-2265. *This long-time tool manufacturer sells wholesale and to schools.*

Edward C. Muller, 3646 White Plains Road, Bronx, New York 10467. (212) 881-7270. *Since the turn of the century Muller has been manufacturing tools for photo and wood engraving. The tools will need shortening but are available wholesale and to schools.*

Abroad

T. N. Lawrence and Son, Ltd., Bleeding Heart Yard, Greville Street, London, England EC1N 8SL. *Even though this company does not sell by mail to the United States, I am including it here so that readers traveling to London will not miss the opportunity to pay this venerable firm a visit. They have been supplying boxwood and other end-grains to wood engravers for nearly a century through three generations of Lawrences. The present owner, the son of "and Son," is now eighty years of age.*

Print Clubs and Societies

This list is incomplete but it will give you an idea of the active societies. Write for membership and exhibition information.

The Boston Printmakers. Sylvia Rantz, Secretary. 299 High Rock Street, Needham, Massachusetts 02192.

Brand Library Art Center. 1601 West Mountain Street, Glendale, California 91201.

Hunterdon Art Center. Anne Steele Marsh, Chairman of Prints. 7 Center Street, Clinton, New Jersey 08809.

International Print Society. Franny Geirhaas, Director. P.O. Box 323, New Hope, Pennsylvania 18938.

Princeton Art Association. Rosedale Road, Princeton, New Jersey 08540.

Print and Drawing Council of Canada. John K. Esler. c/o University of Calgary, 2920 24th Avenue, N.W., Calgary, Alberta, Canada 1814.

The Print Club. Attention, Nancy Boylen. 1614 Latimer Street, Philadelphia, Pennsylvania 19103.

The Print Club of Albany, Inc. Alice Pauline Schafer, President. 33 Hawthorne Avenue, Albany, New York 12203.

The Printmaking Council of New Jersey. Box 964, Plainfield, New Jersey 06061.

Society of American Graphic Artists. 1083 Fifth Avenue, New York, New York 10028.

Society of Wood Engravers and Relief Printers. 10 Sunningdale Avenue, Eastcote, Ruislip, Middlesex, England.

Summit Art Center. 68 Elm Street, Summit, New Jersey 07901.

Yellowstone Print Club (Print Collectors Group). 401 North 27th Street, Billings, Montana 59101.

Print Exhibitions

This is about one-third the number of annual print shows in the United States, but once you enter one of them, you find yourself on the mailing lists of all the others. Good luck.

Annual Cedar City National Art Exhibition. Cedar City Art Committee. Thomas A. Leek, Chairman. c/o Braithwaite Fine Arts Gallery, Southern Utah State College, Cedar City, Utah 84720.

Annual National Print and Drawing Exhibition. Oklahoma Art Center. Attention, M. K. Connery. 3113 Pershing Boulevard, Oklahoma City, Oklahoma 73107.

Annual Prints, Drawing and Crafts Exhibition. The Arkansas Arts Center. Attention, Townsend Wolfe, Director. MacArthur Park, P.O. Box 2137, Little Rock, Arkansas 72203.

Bradley National Print and Drawing Exhibition. School of Art. Attention, W. A. S. Hatch. Bradley University, Peoria, Illinois 61625.

Boston Printmakers National Boston Exhibition. c/o S. M. Rantz. 299 High Rock Street, Department A, Needham, Massachusetts 02102.

Boston Printmakers/Decordova Museum Printmakers. Decordova Museum, Sandy Pond Road, Lincoln, Massachusetts 01773.

Dulin Gallery of Art National Print and Drawing Competition. Dulin Gallery of Art, 3100 Kingston Pike, Knoxville, Tennessee 37919.

The Georgia Tech Student Center. Annual National Dogwood Festival Art Show. Georgia Institute of Technology, Atlanta, Georgia 30332.

Hunterdon Art Center National Print Exhibition. Attention, Anne Steele March. Hunterdon Art Center, 7 Center Street, Clinton, New Jersey 08809.

Miami University Prints and Drawings. V.A.C. Department of Art. Miami University, Oxford, Ohio 45056.

Midwestern Printing and Drawing Competition. Keith M. Edwards, Coordinator. Tulsa City Library, 400 Civic Center, Tulsa. Oklahoma 74103.

Pratt Graphics Center. International Miniature Print Competition and Exhibition. Attention Pauline Kwartler. 831 Broadway, New York, New York 10003.

Small Print Exhibition. Department of Creative Arts. Creative Arts 1, Purdue University, West Lafayette, Indiana 47907.

Books for Further Reference

Some of the books on this list are long out of print, but I include them here because they are worthy source books and I have found all of them at one time or another in secondhand book shops and you may do the same.

Historical Works

A History of Wood Engraving by Douglas Percy Bliss. London: Spring Books, 1928; reprinted in 1964.

A Brief History of Wood-Engraving from Its Invention by Joseph Cundall. London: Sampson Low, Marston & Company, 1895.

Early American Book Illustrators and Wood Engravers 1670–1810. Vols. 1 and 2. Princeton, N.J.: Princeton University Press, 1968. A complete list with biographical and bibliographical material of wood engravers covering the first hundred years of the art in America. An essential guide for the historian.

American Prints from Wood: An Exhibition of Woodcuts and Wood Engravings. Organized by Jane M. Farmer. Washington, D.C.: Smithsonian Institution Travel Exhibition Service, 1975. An excellent exhibition catalogue available directly from the Smithsonian.

The Modern Woodcut by Herbert Furst. New York: Dodd Mead & Company, 1924.

The Woodcut of Today at Home and Abroad. Edited by Geoffrey Holme. London: The Studio Ltd., 1927.

1800 Woodcuts by Thomas Bewick and His School. Introduction by Robert Hutchinson. New York: Dover Publications, 1962.

Wood Engraving of the 1930s. Edited by Clare Leighton. London: The Studio Ltd., 1936 (Special Winter Number).

The Woodblock Engravers by Kenneth Lindley. New York: Drake Publishers, Inc., 1972. A history of the anonymous commercial product illustrators of the nineteenth century.

The New Book-Illustration in France by Leon Pichon. Translated by H. B. Grinsditch. London, The Studio Ltd., 1924.

Wood Engravings by Thomas Bewick. Introduction by John Raynor. London: Penguin Books Ltd., 1947.

The New Woodcut by Malcolm C. Salaman. London: The Studio Ltd., 1930.

Thomas Bewick by Montague Weekly. London: Oxford University Press, 1953.

Technical Works

The Craft of Woodcuts by John R. Biggs. London: Blanford Press, 1963.

The Way of Wood Engraving by Dorothea Braby. London: The Studio Publications, 1953.

Graven Image: An Autobiographical Textbook by John Farleigh. London: Macmillan & Co., 1940.

A Woodcut Manual by J. J. Lankes. New York: Henry Holt and Company, 1932.

Wood Engraving and Woodcuts by Clare Leighton. London and New York: The Studio Publications, 1932; revised edition, 1944.

The Wood Engravings of Joan Hassall. Introduction by Ruari McLean. London: Oxford University Press, 1960.

How I Make Woodcuts and Wood Engravings by Hans Alexander Mueller. New York: American Artists Group, Inc., 1945.

The Technique of Wood Engraving by John O'Connor. New York: Watson Guptill Publications, 1971. London: Batsford Ltd., 1971.

Works Illustrated with Wood Engravings

The books listed here range from children's books and the classics to surveys of the work of individual engravers; all contain engravings that will instruct and inspire both beginner and veteran engravers.

My Village, Sturbridge by Gary Bowen. Engravings by Randy Miller. New York: Farrar, Straus & Giroux, 1977.

Wuthering Heights by Emily Bronte. Engravings by Fritz Eichenberg. New York: Random House, 1943.

Don Quixote de la Mancha, Part One, by Miguel de Cervantes Saavedra. Translated by Peter Motteux. Engravings by Hans Alexander Mueller. New York: Random House, 1941.

They Walk in the Night by Elizabeth Coatsworth. Engravings by Stefan Martin. New York: W. W. Norton & Co., Inc., 1969.

The Sparrow Bush by Elizabeth Coatsworth. Engravings by Stefan Martin. New York: W. W. Norton & Co., Inc., 1966.

A Medieval Bestiary. Translated and introduced by T. J. Elliott. Engravings by Gillian Tyler. Boston: Godine, 1971.

The Wood Engravings of Robert Gibbings. Edited by Patience Empson. Chicago: Quadrangle Books, 1959.

Wood Engravings and Drawings of Iain Macnab of Barachastlain by Albert Garrett. Tunbridge Wells, England: Midas Books, 1973.

Modern Belgian Wood Engravers by Jan-Albert Goris. New York: Belgian Government Information Center, 1949.

Ghosts and Spirits of Many Lands. Edited by Freya Littledale. Engravings by Stefan Martin. New York: Doubleday & Company, Inc., 1970.

Passionate Journey: A Novel in Woodcuts by Frans Masereel. New York: Dover Publications, Inc., 1971. Reprint of the 1920 novel published in Munich. Although not wood engraving, it is worth examining because it will give you an idea of what a novel in pictures was. It is also readily available, whereas the works of Ward and Nückel (listed below) are not.

Woodcuts of New York by Hans Alexander Mueller. New York: J. J. Augustin, 1938.

Nicole's Guide to Paris by Société d'Edition du Nicole's Guide, Paris. Prefaces by Louis Bromfield and Jean Cocteau. Engravings by Armanelli. New York: A. De Milly, 1951. Many multicolored wood engravings that resemble the watercolors from which they were made.

Destiny: A Novel in Pictures by Otto Nückel. New York: Farrar & Rinehart, Inc., 1930.

A Selection of Wood Engravings by Imre Reiner. Chicago: Apprentice House, 1964.

The Adventures of the Black Girl in Her Search for God by Bernard Shaw. Engravings by John Farleigh. New York: Dodd, Mead & Company, 1933.

A Felicity of Carols by Helen Siegl. Barre, Mass.: Barre Publishing, Inc., 1970.

A Zaddick Christ: A Suite of Wood Engravings by Bernard A Solomon. Greenwood, S.C.: The Attic Press, Inc., 1973.

Small Pond by Marguerite Walters. Engravings by Stefan Martin. New York: E. P. Dutton & Co., Inc., 1967.

Mad Man's Drum: A Novel in Woodcuts by Lynd Ward. New York: Jonathan Cape and Harrison Smith, Inc., 1930.

Also by Lynd Ward: *God's Man: A Novel in Woodcuts.* New York: Jonathan Cape and Harrison Smith, 1929. Reissued by St. Martin's Press, 1978. Although Ward's subtitles refer to "woodcuts," these are actually wood engravings.

Rockwellkentiana by R. K. Zigrosser and Carl Zigrosser. Engravings by Rockwell Kent. New York: Harcourt, Brace and Company, 1933.

Works for the Collector

Memorial Edition of Thomas Bewick's Works. Vol. I: *British Birds* (land birds); Vol. II: *British Birds* (water birds); Vol. III: *Quadrupeds;* Vol. IV: *The Fables of Aesop;* Vol. V: *Memoir.* London: Bernard Quaritch, 1887. These are the five major works by Thomas Bewick. Today, even the copies of this memorial edition can only be found in rare bookstores.

A Treatise on Wood Engraving by John Jackson. London: Chatto and Windus, c. 1839; revised and reprinted, 1861. Definitive history of wood engraving to midcentury, written by one of Thomas Bewick's students.

Index

(Page numbers in italics refer to illustrations)